Vintage Nudes of Yesteryear

by Carl Scott Harker

An Aldouspi Publication

Table of Contents

Introduction

For most of our recorded history, artists - painters and illustrators - were the only source of images featuring the female nude. Sometimes these nude portraits were presented very realistically, sometimes idealized and almost always beautifully. Today, we still have many artists creating new works presenting nude images of women.

Then along came the camera and a whole new way to present the female nude was born. And suddenly anyone could be portrayed in the nude without the usual interpretation and the cost of using artists. Ironically, though, the first nudes shot in the early 1850's were mostly used by painters in lieu of live models, but the general public quickly showed its interest in these more accessible images.

By the early 1900's, professional photographers, artists in their own right, had broken through most of the social taboos regarding nudity and more and more photos of naked women were being presented to the viewing and buying public. In this book, you will find vintage examples of those nudes, that both shocked and titillated the public when first seen. These images come from magazines, art instruction books, "French" postcards and professional shots of models and stage performers.

Unfortunately for us, many photographs from this vintage time have been lost or corroded by time. I have selected what I believe are some of the best images taken by photographers, prior to 1924, for your education and enjoyment.

The photos shown here are were all taken in black and white and are so presented.

Nude Woman Reading Magazine

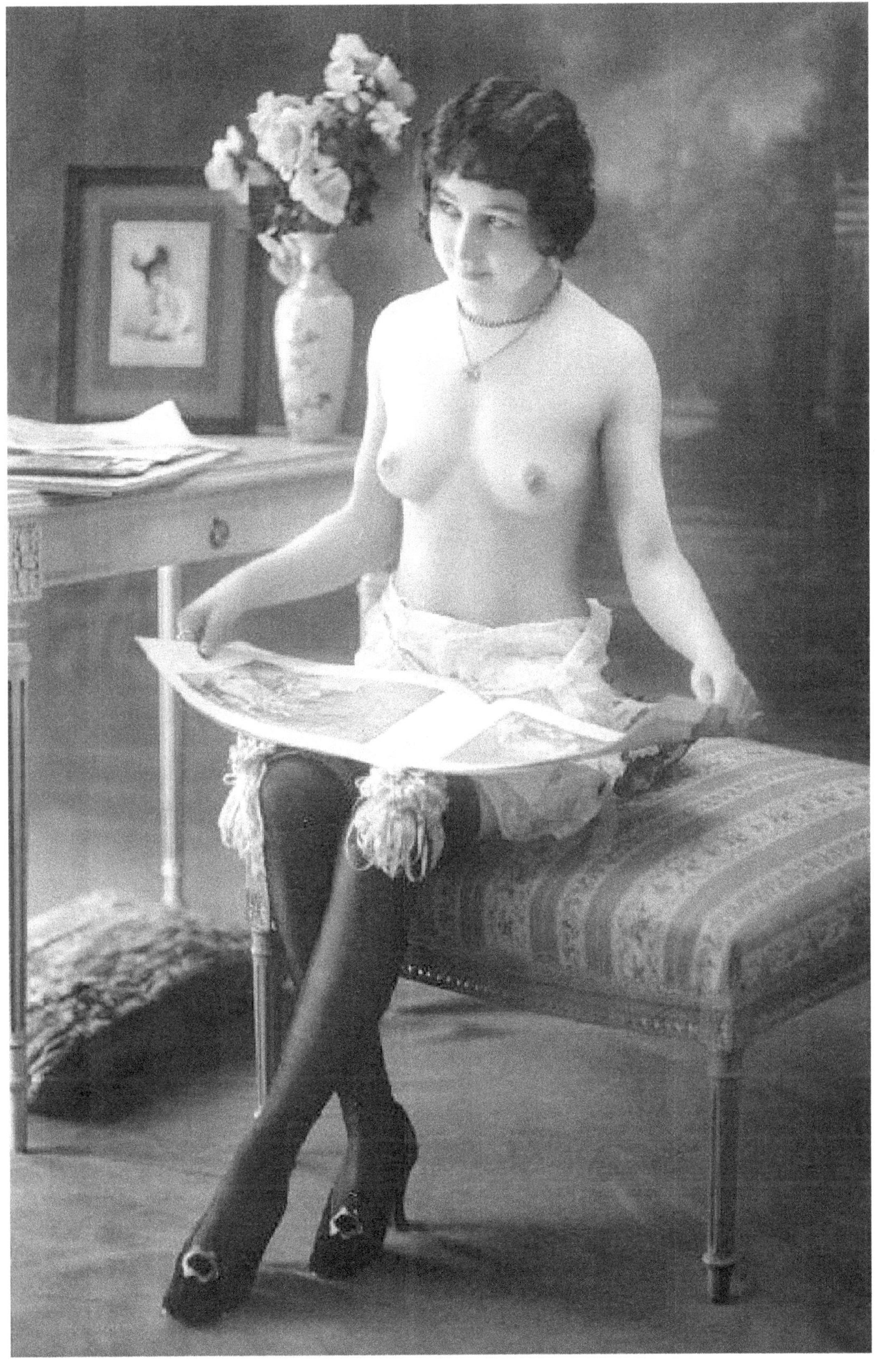

Nude Woman With Pipe

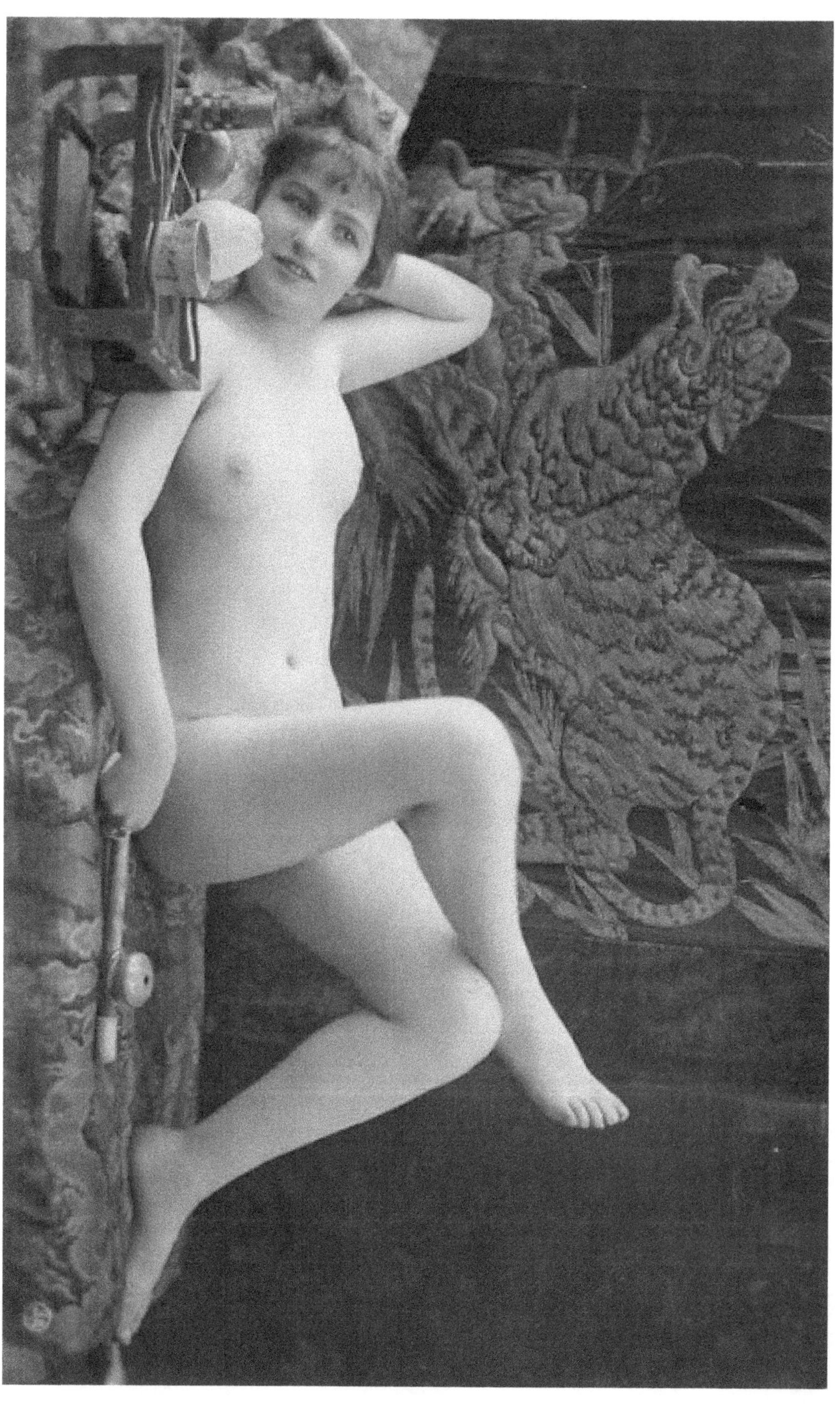

Nude Woman Reflected In Mirror

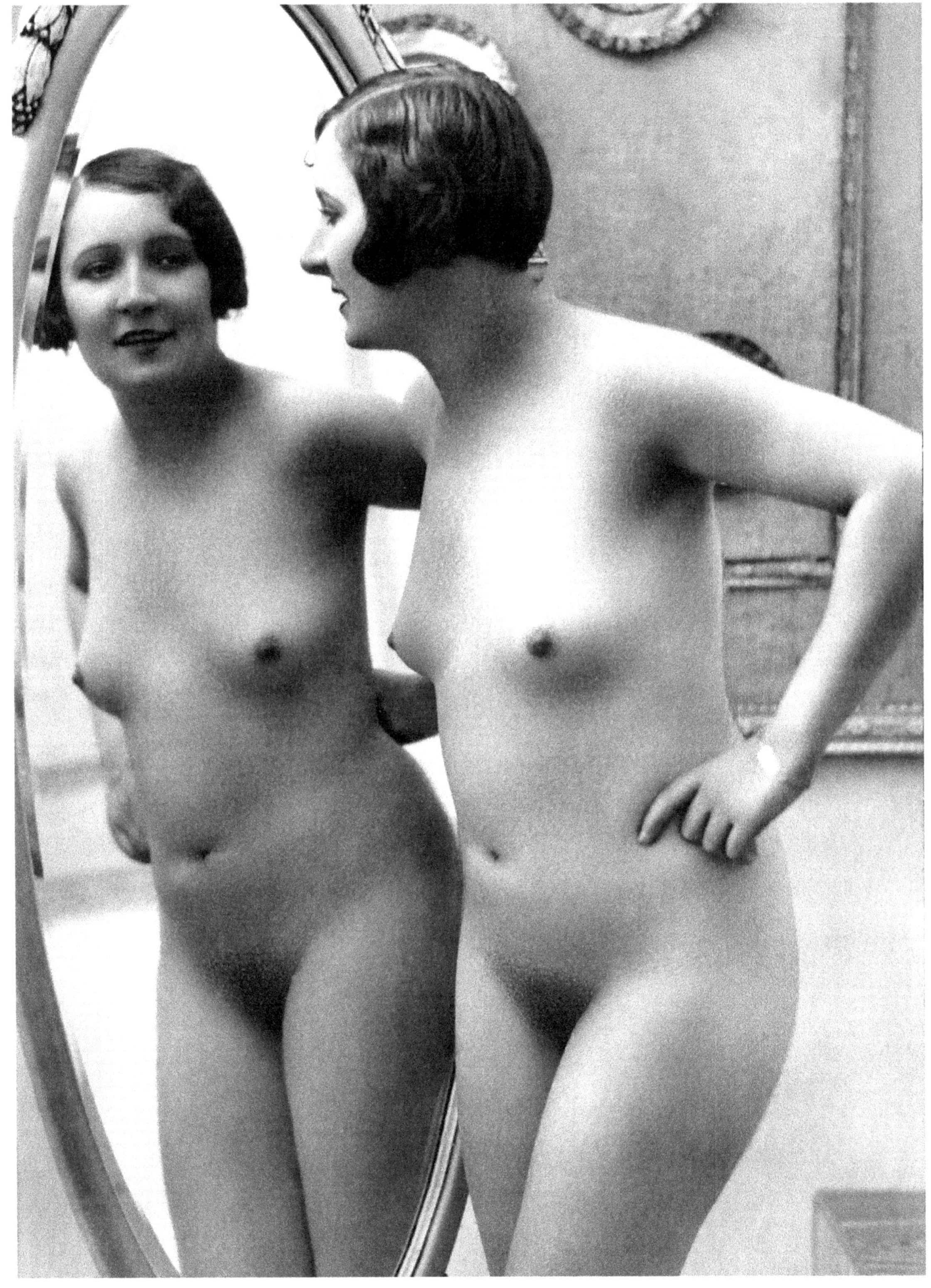

Nude Woman with Hand on Breast

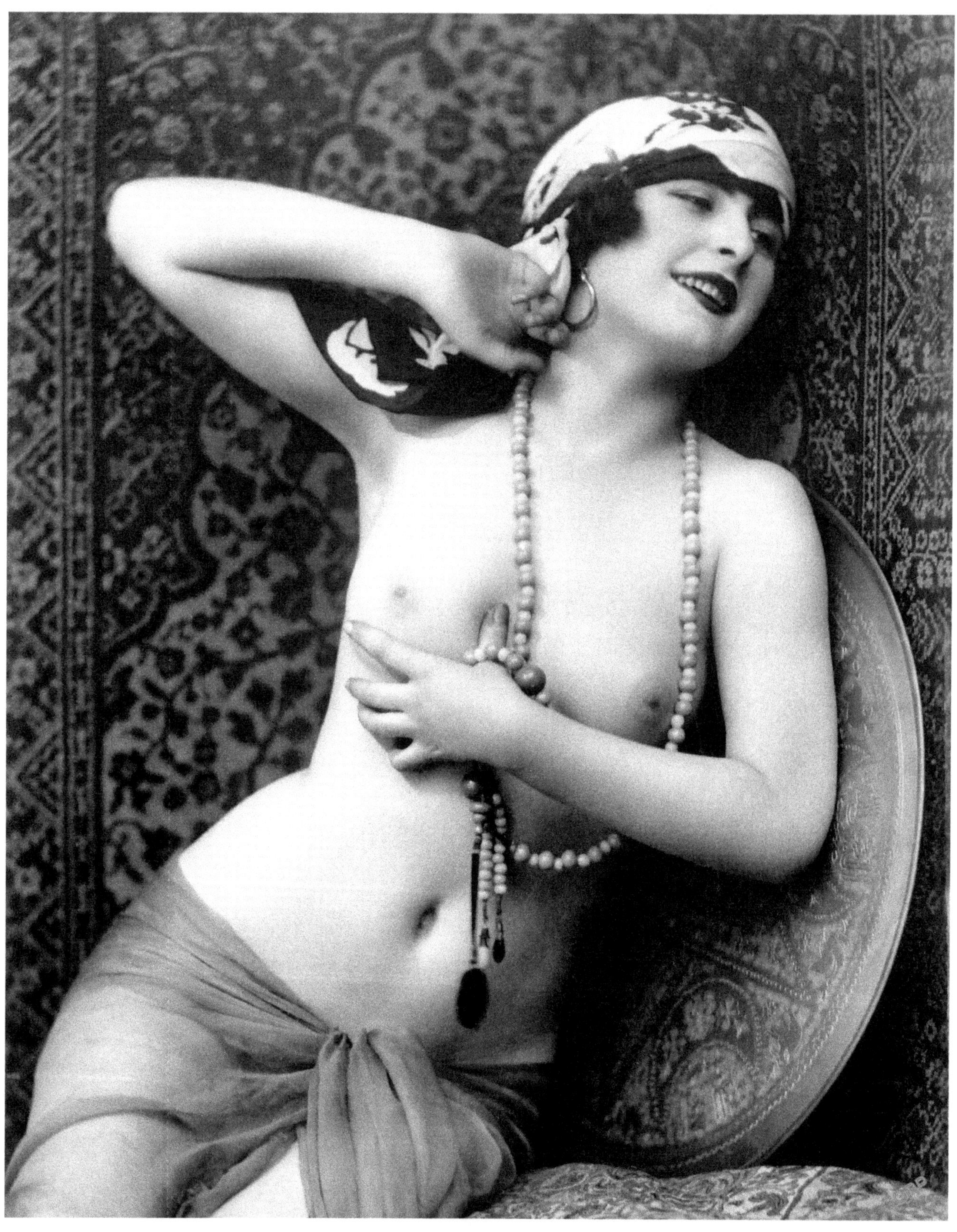

Ghostly Nude Woman

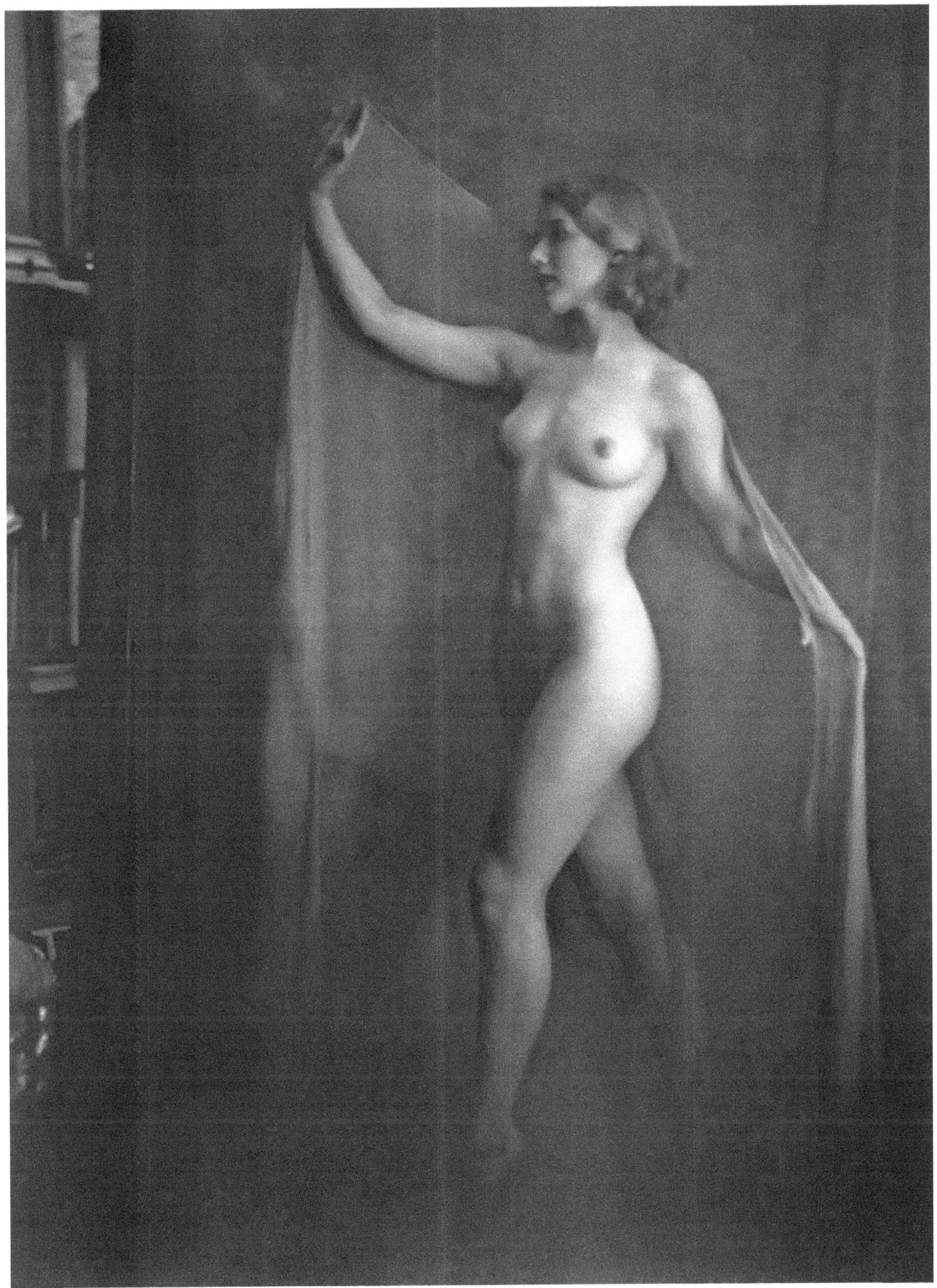

Nude Woman With Dirty Foot

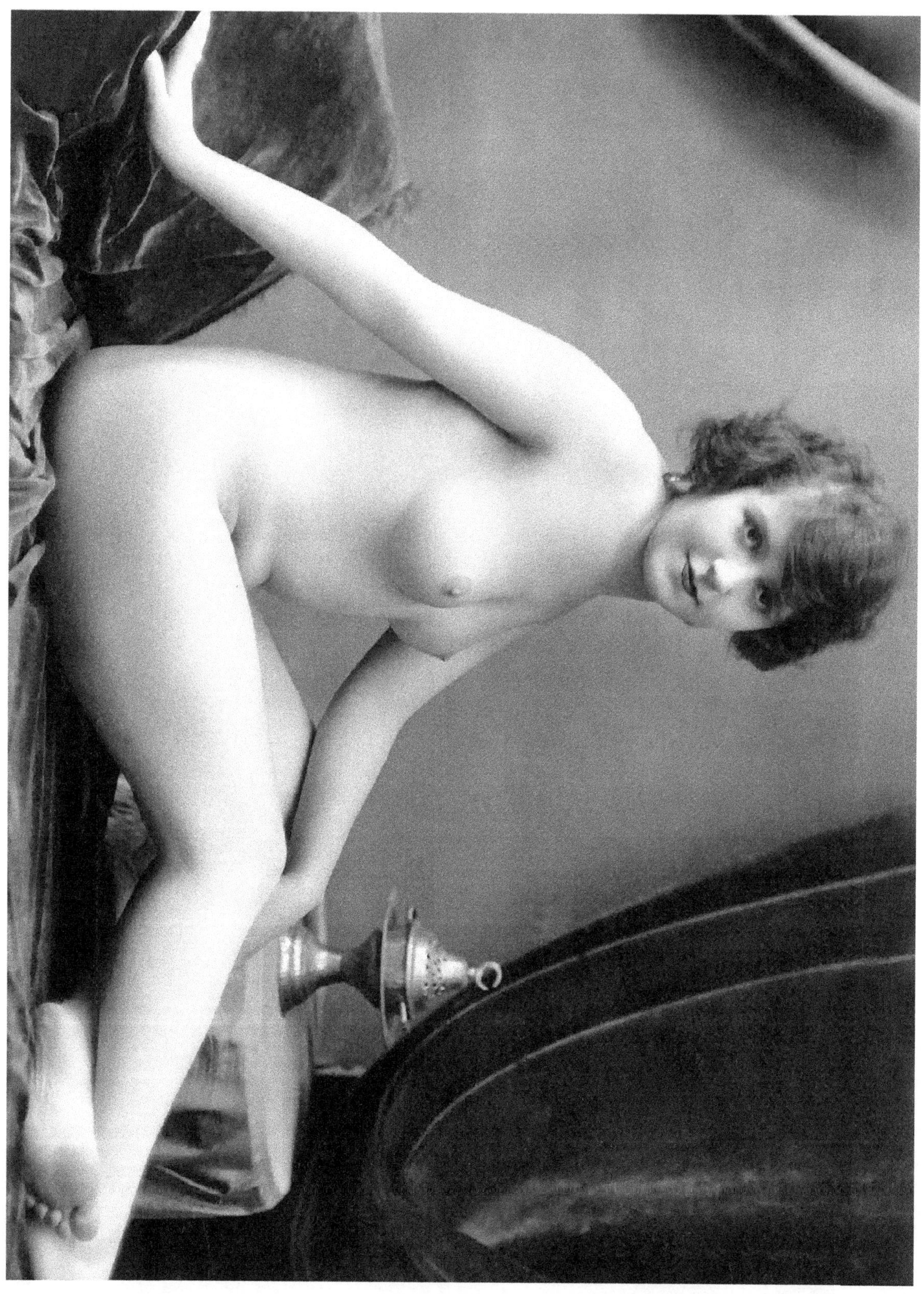

Nude Woman Leaning Against Wall

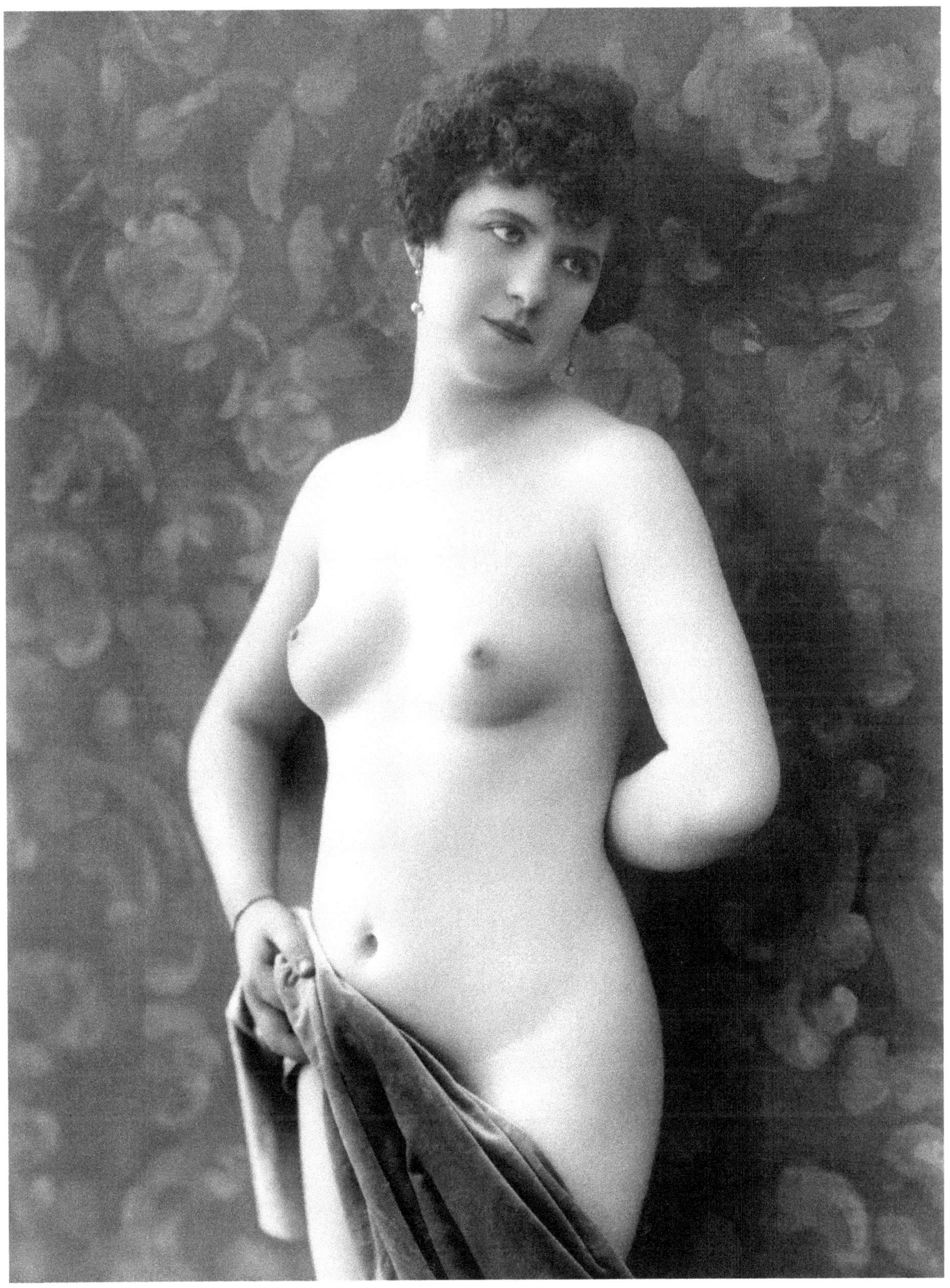

Nude Woman Sitting On a Log

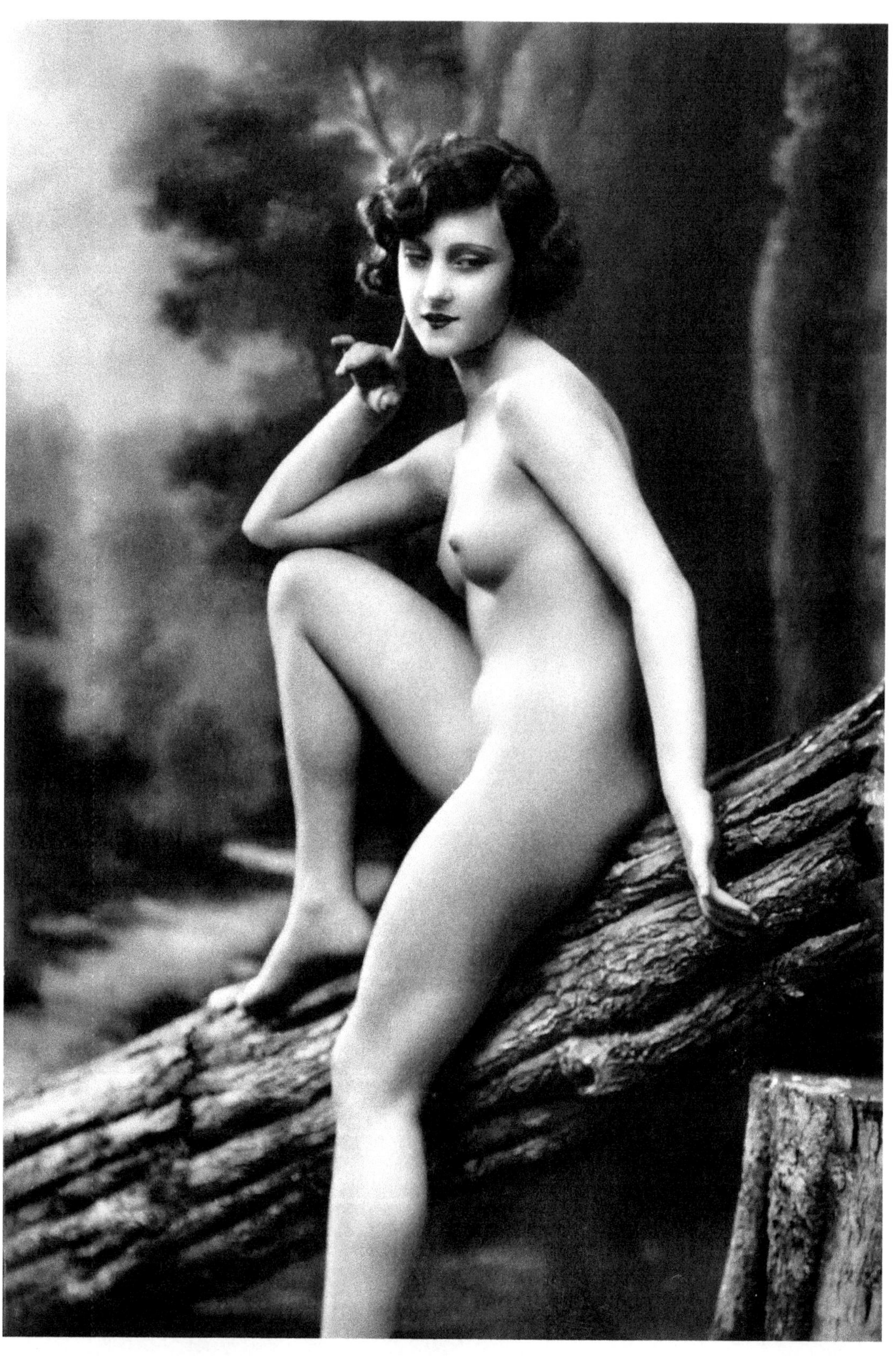

Nude Woman Expecting A Storm

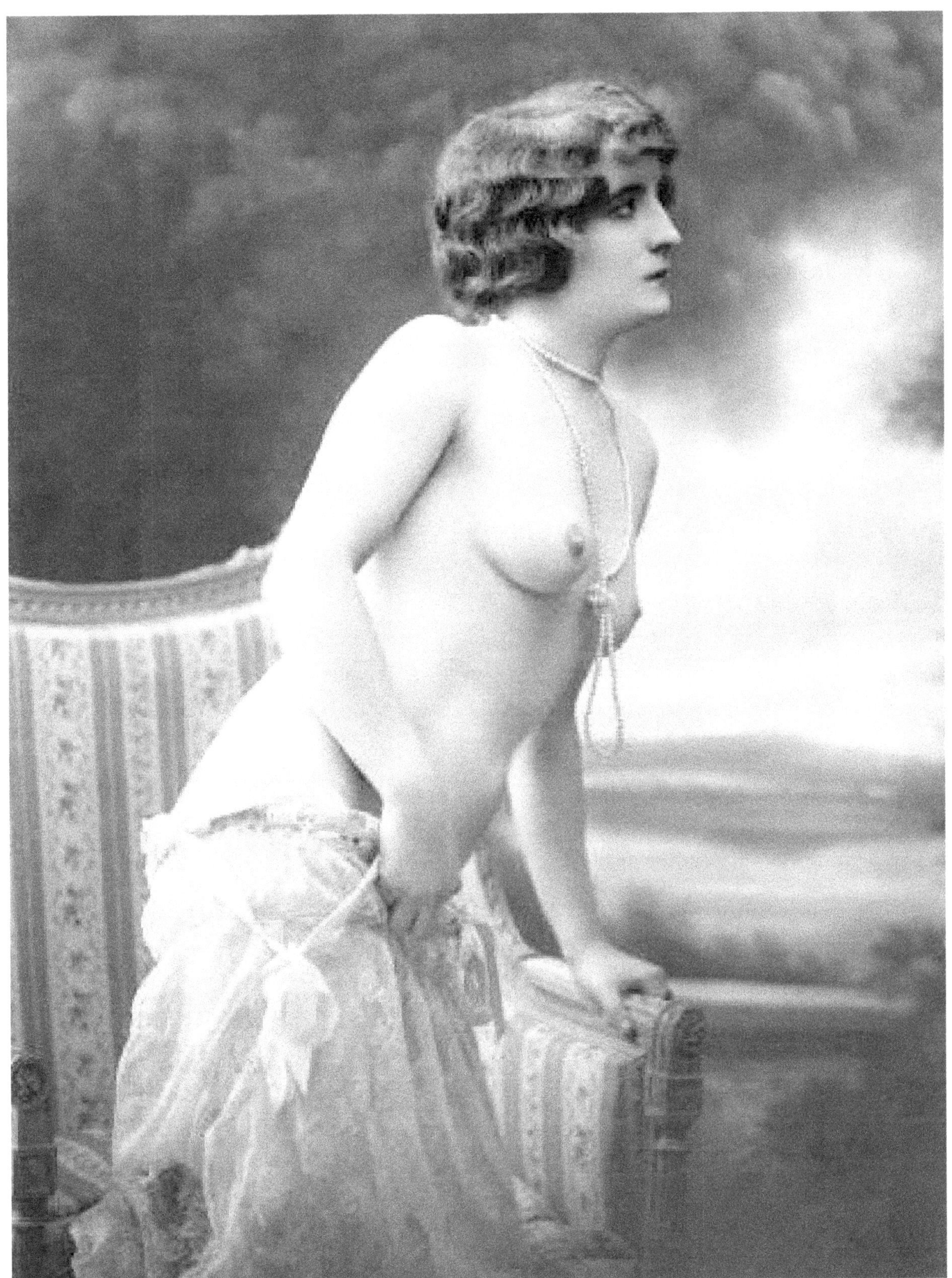

Nude Woman On The Moon

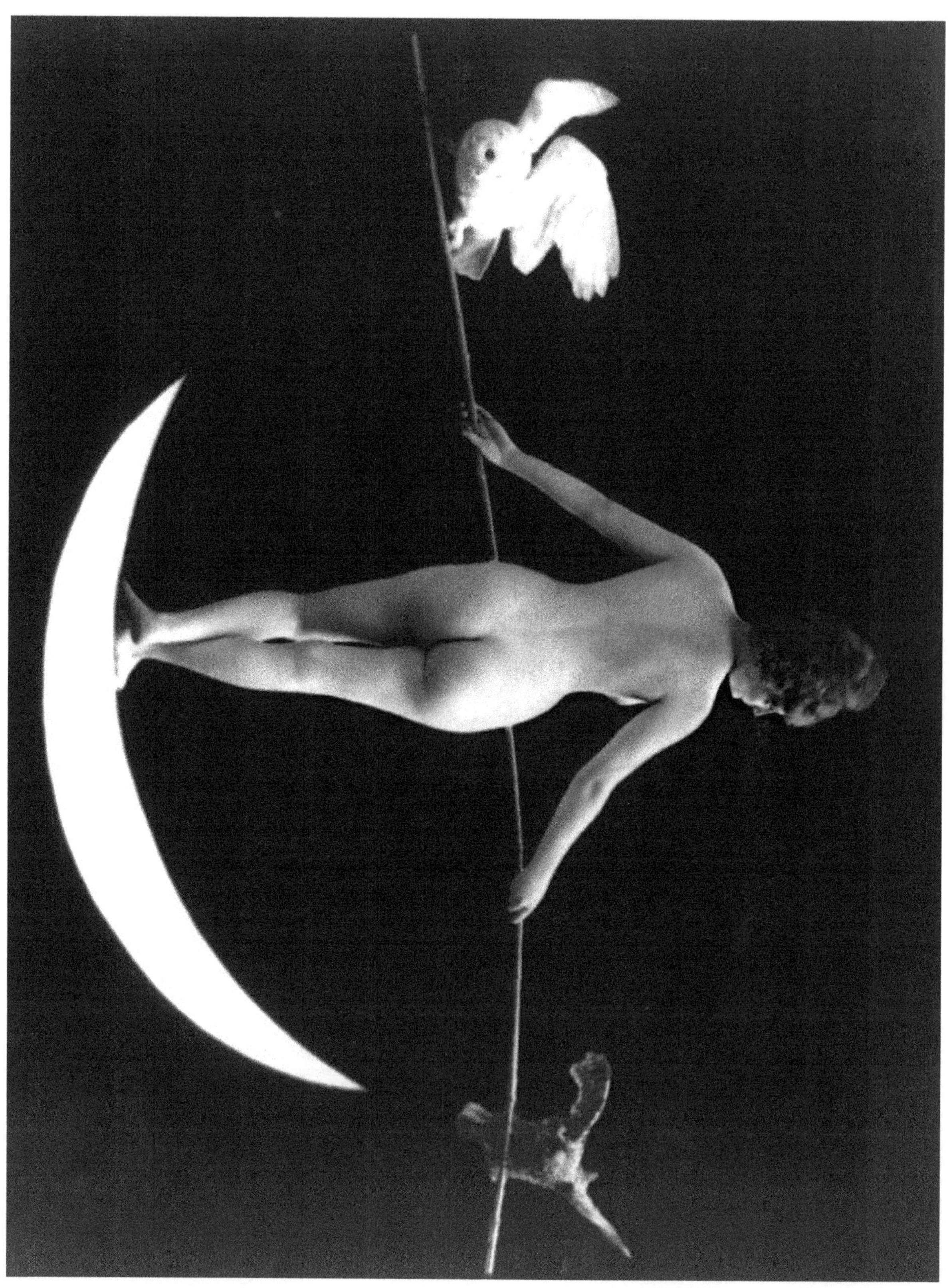

Resting on the Floor on a Pillow

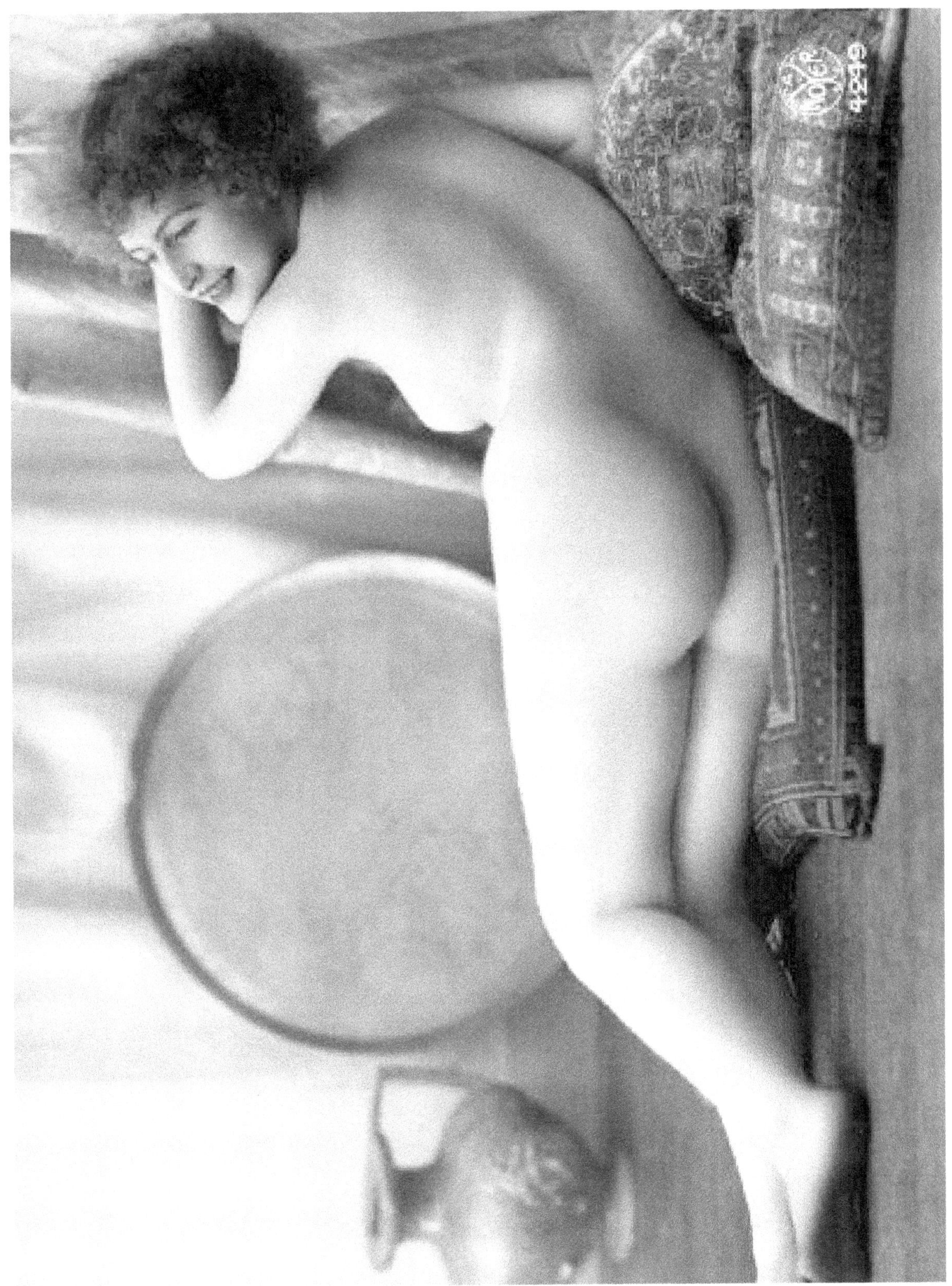

Nude Woman With Perky Breasts

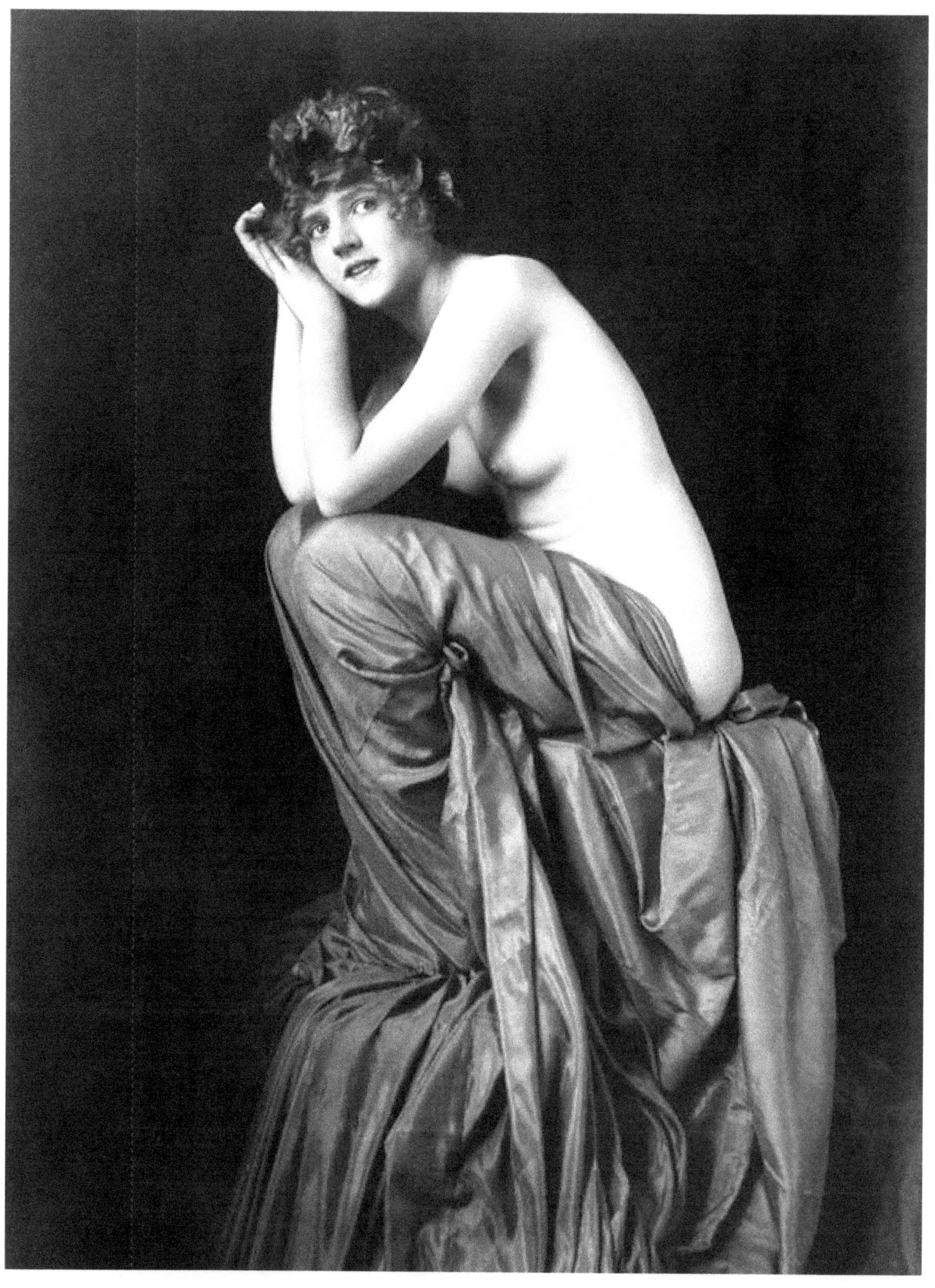

Nude Woman With Violin

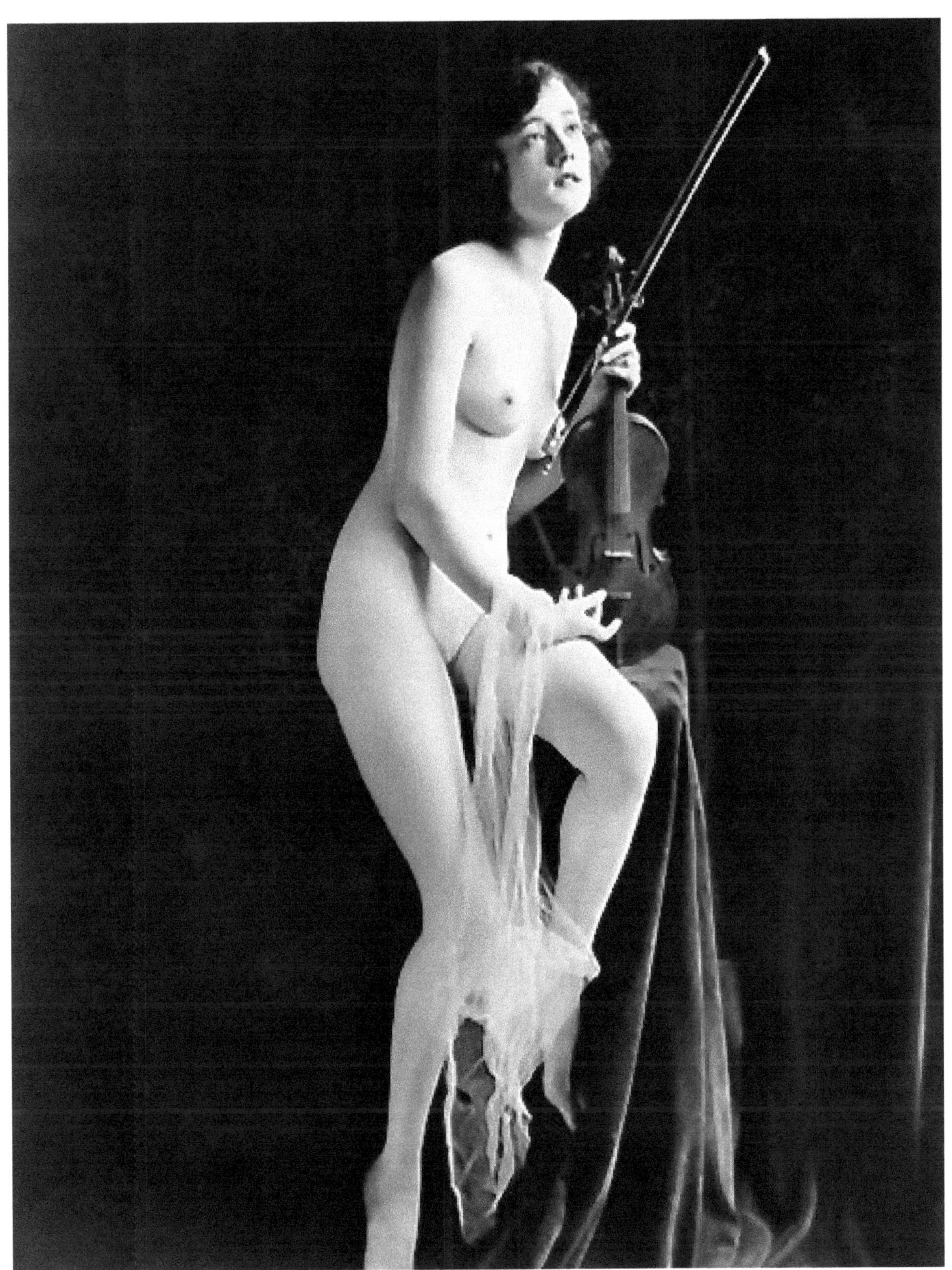

Nude Woman In Front of Curtains

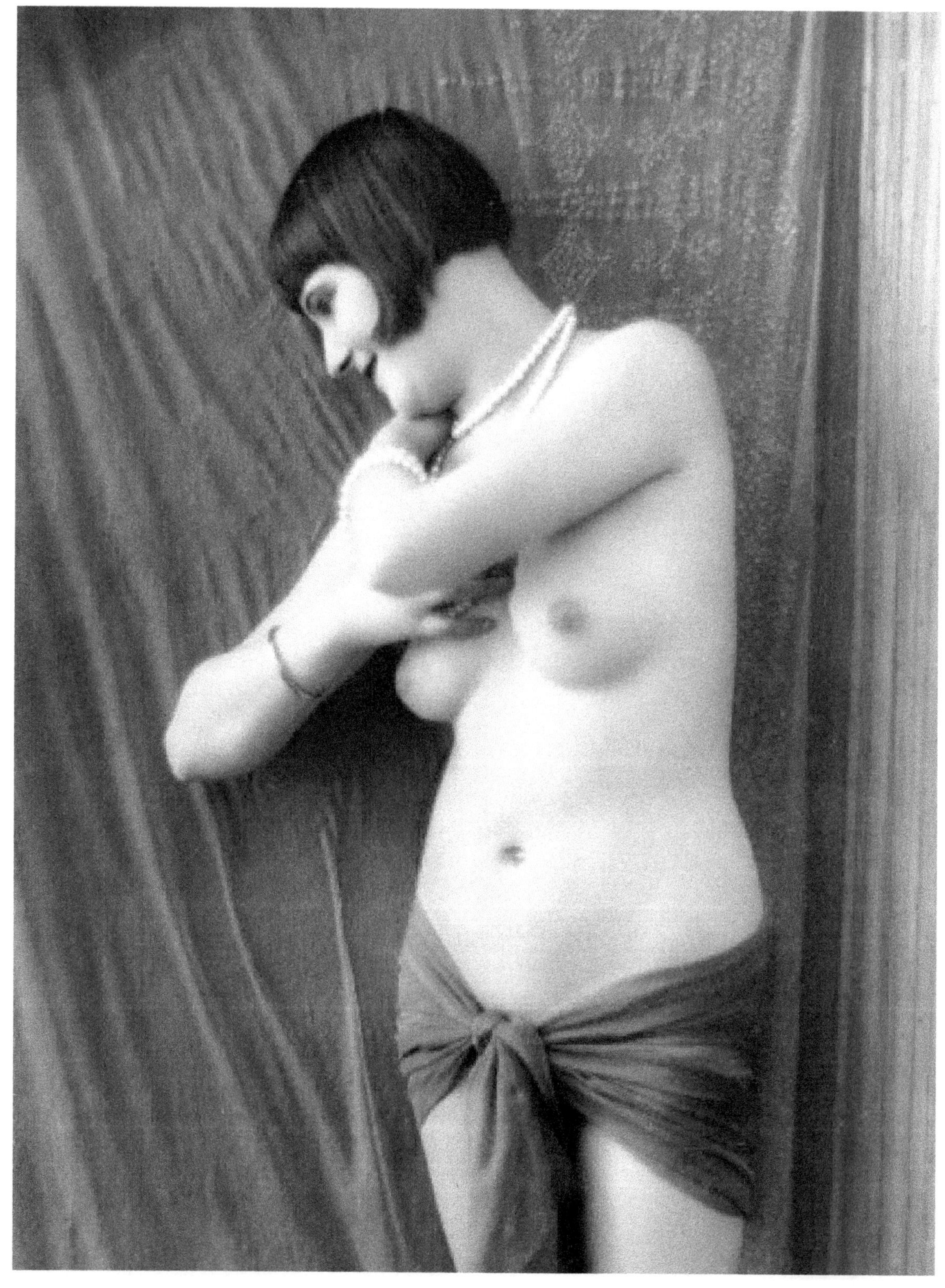

Nude Woman Visiting In a Hotel Room

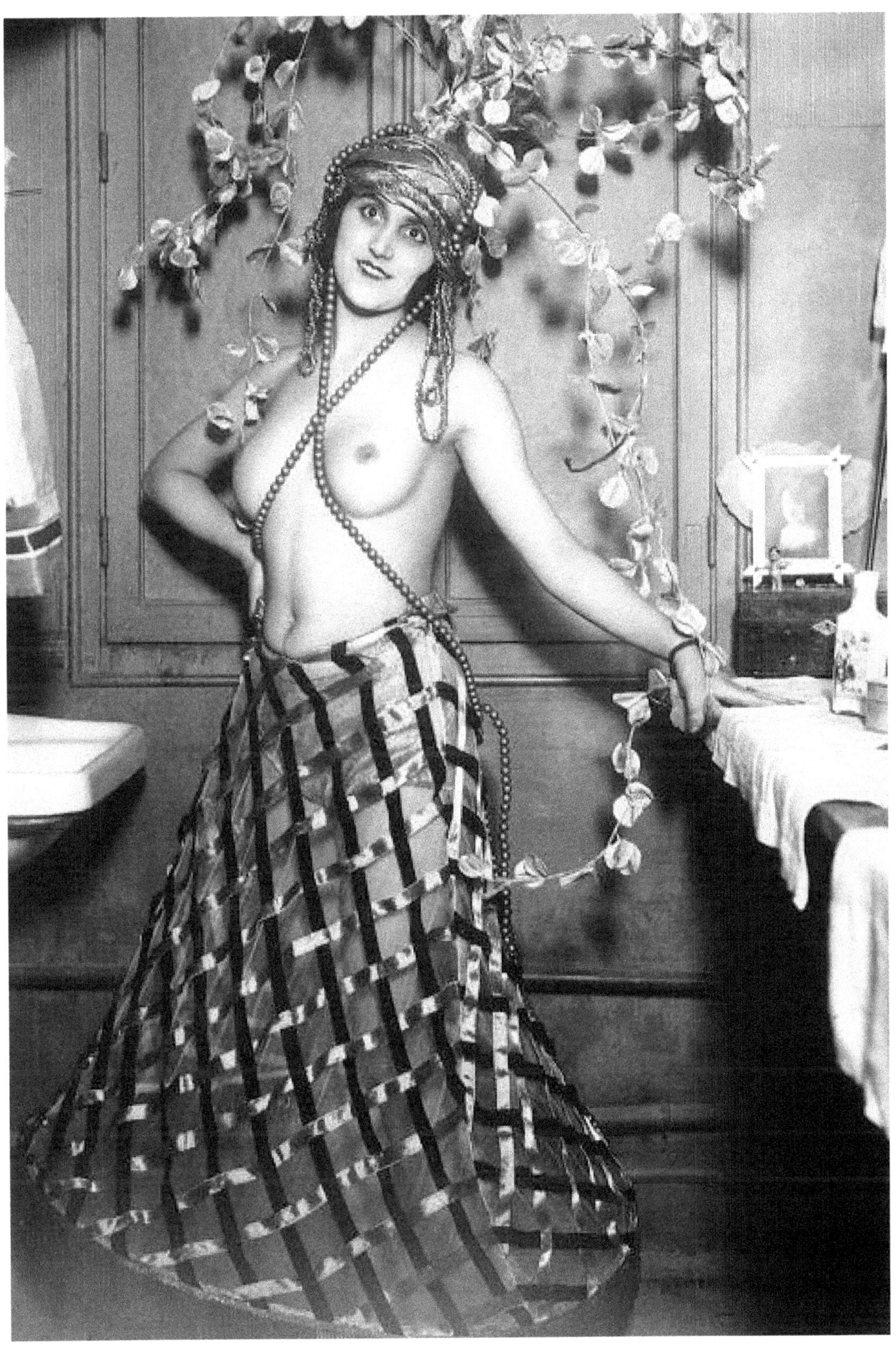

Woman Reveals Her Breasts

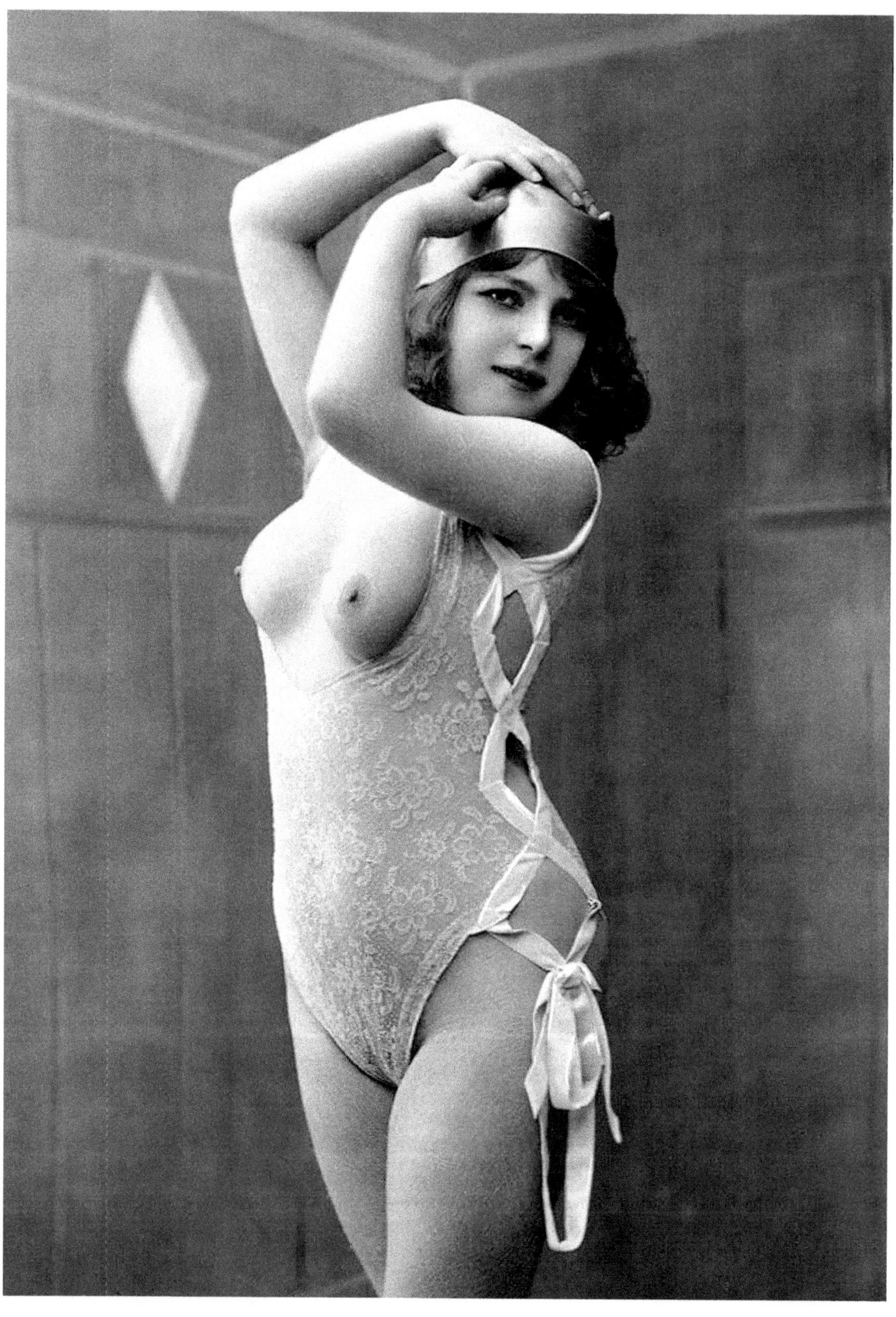

Nude Woman With Cigarette

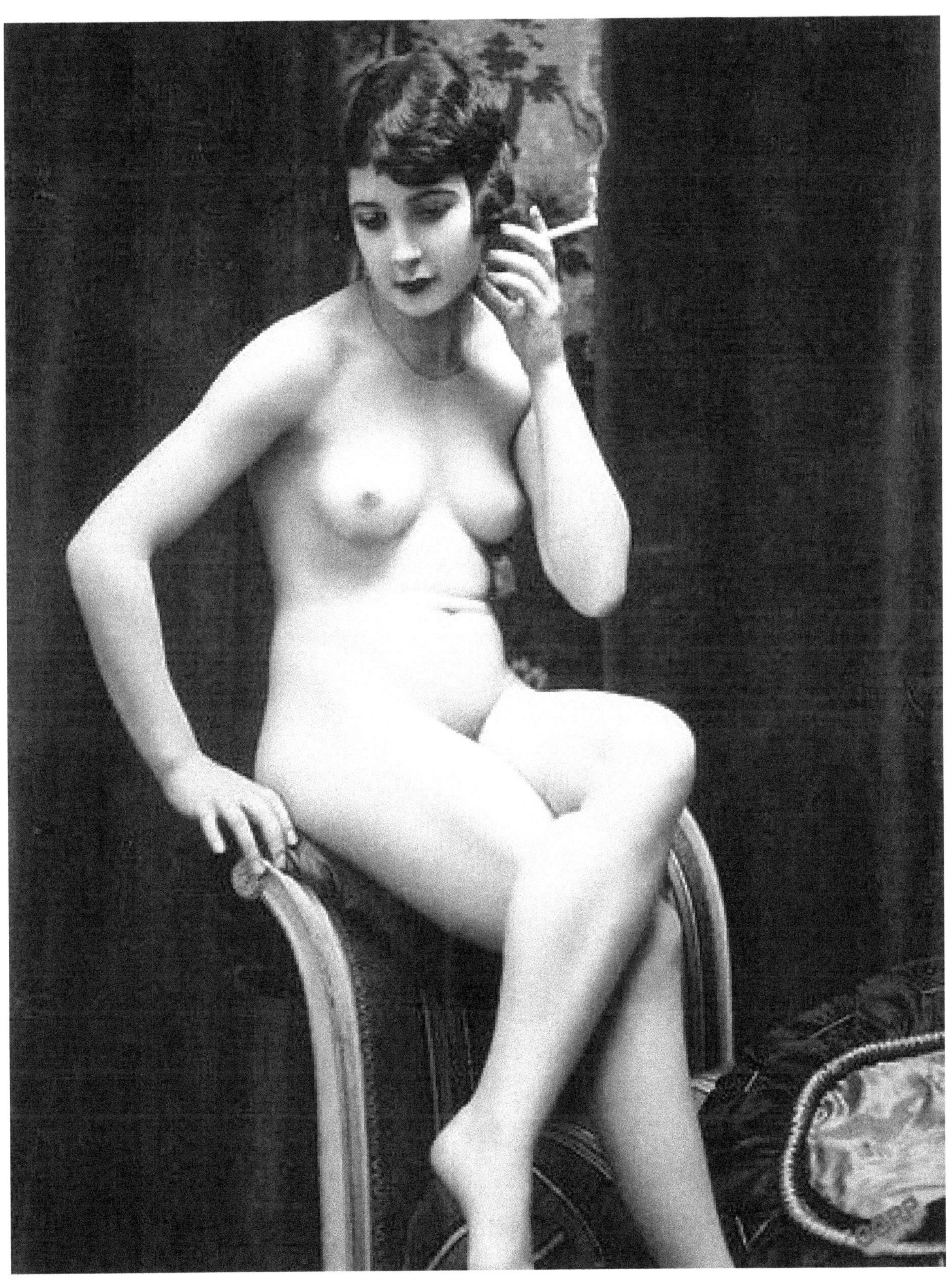

Nude Woman With Angel Wings

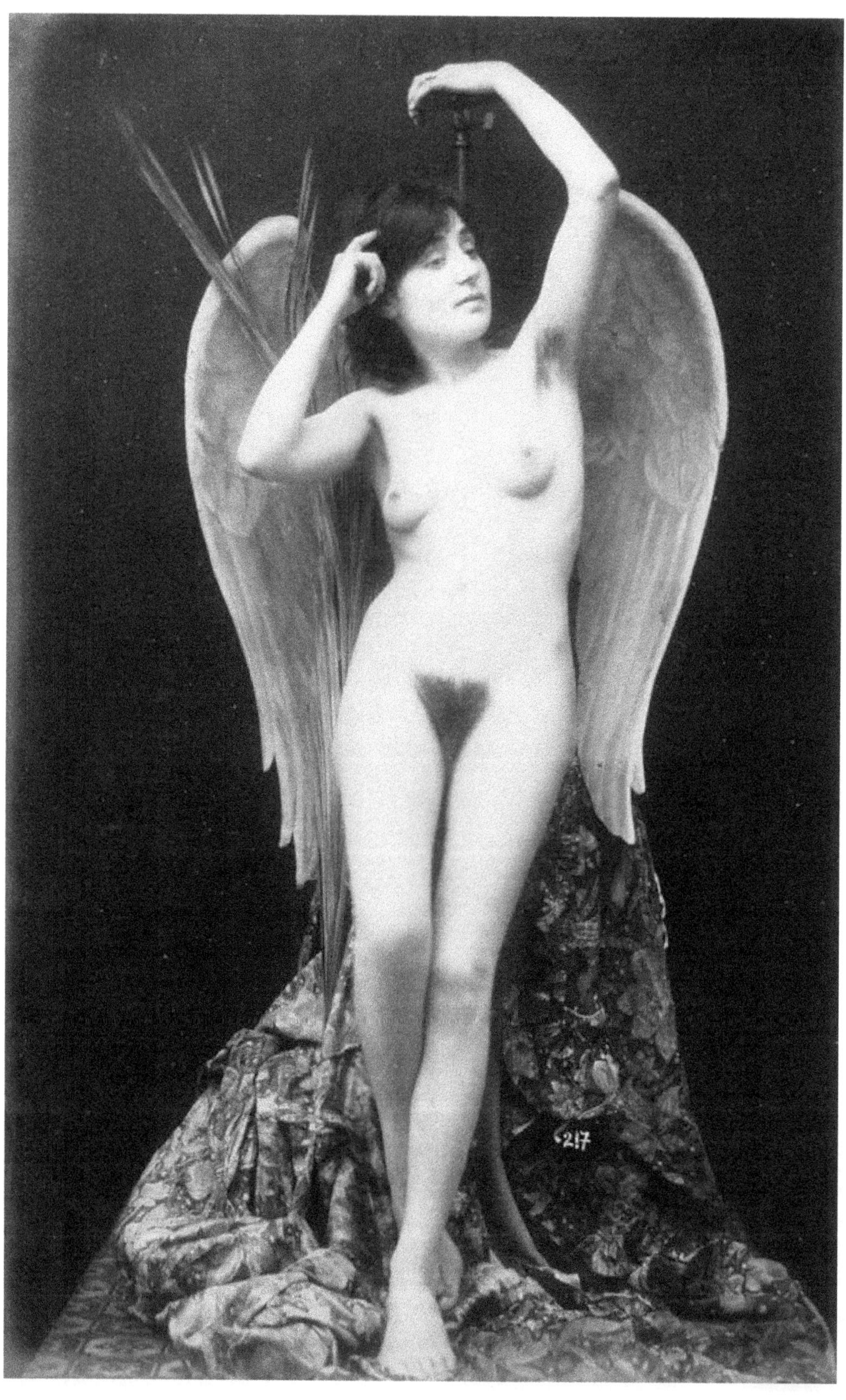

Nude Bedouin Woman

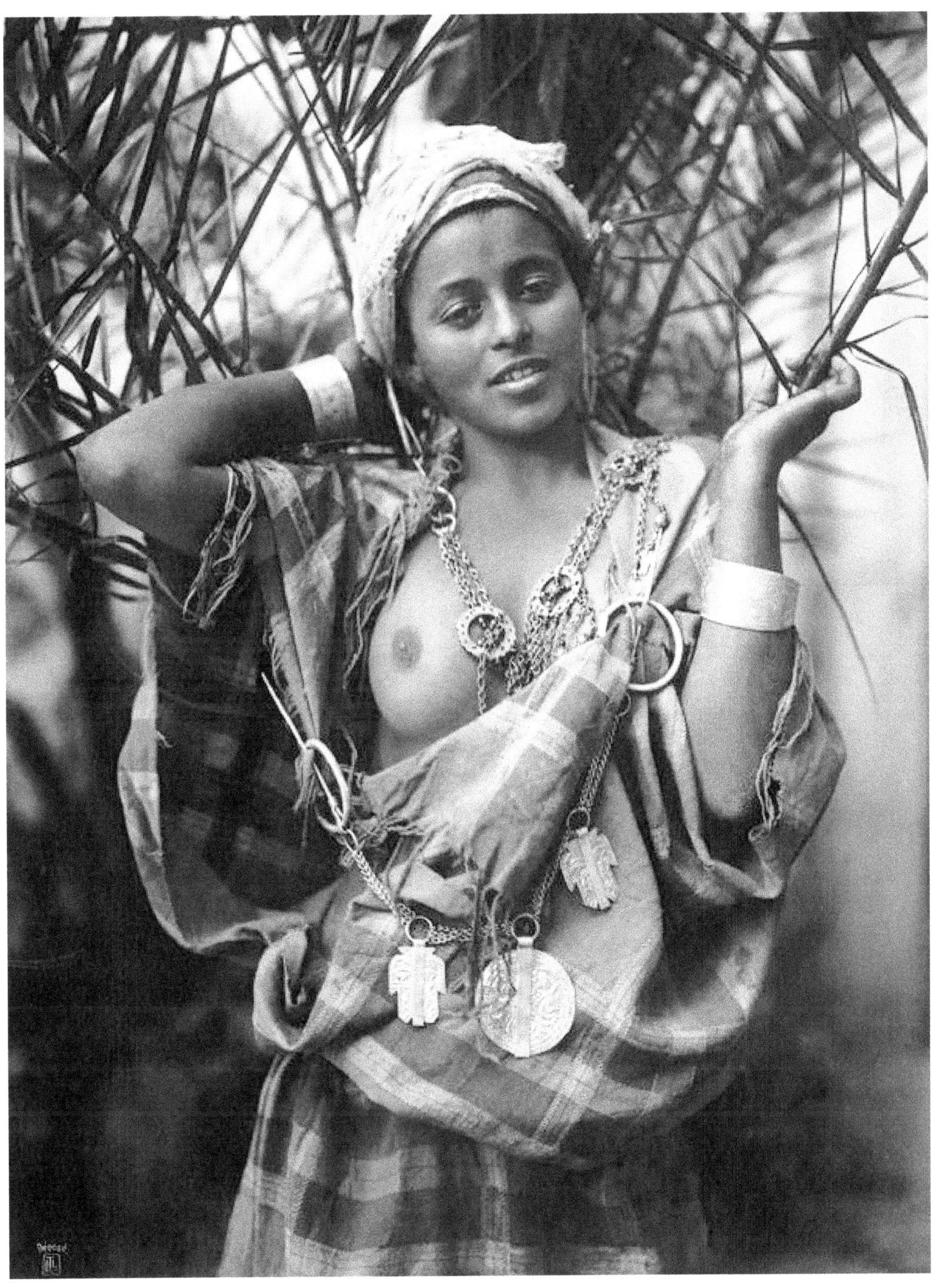

Cute Nude Woman With Hand on Head

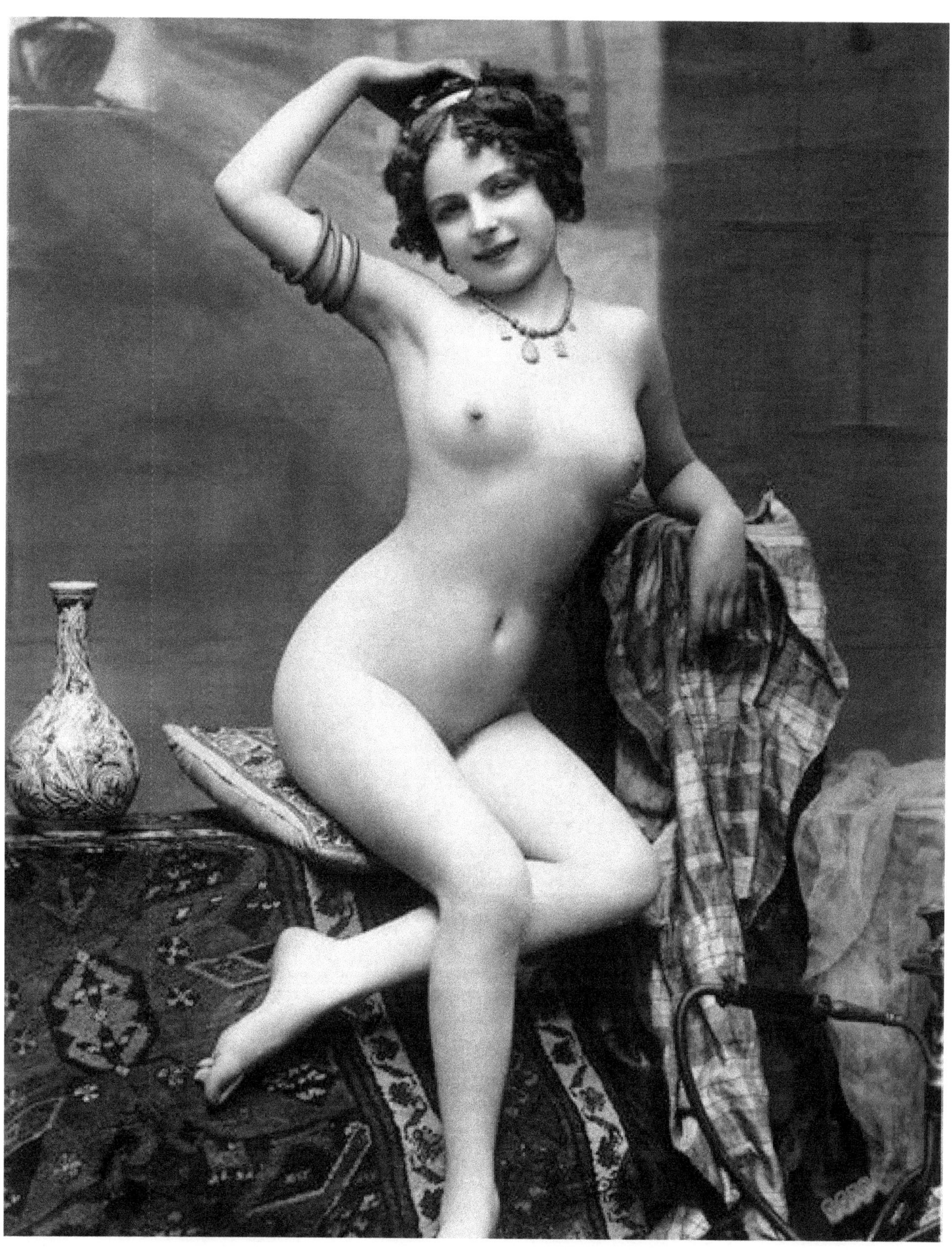

Nude Woman Posed in the Studio

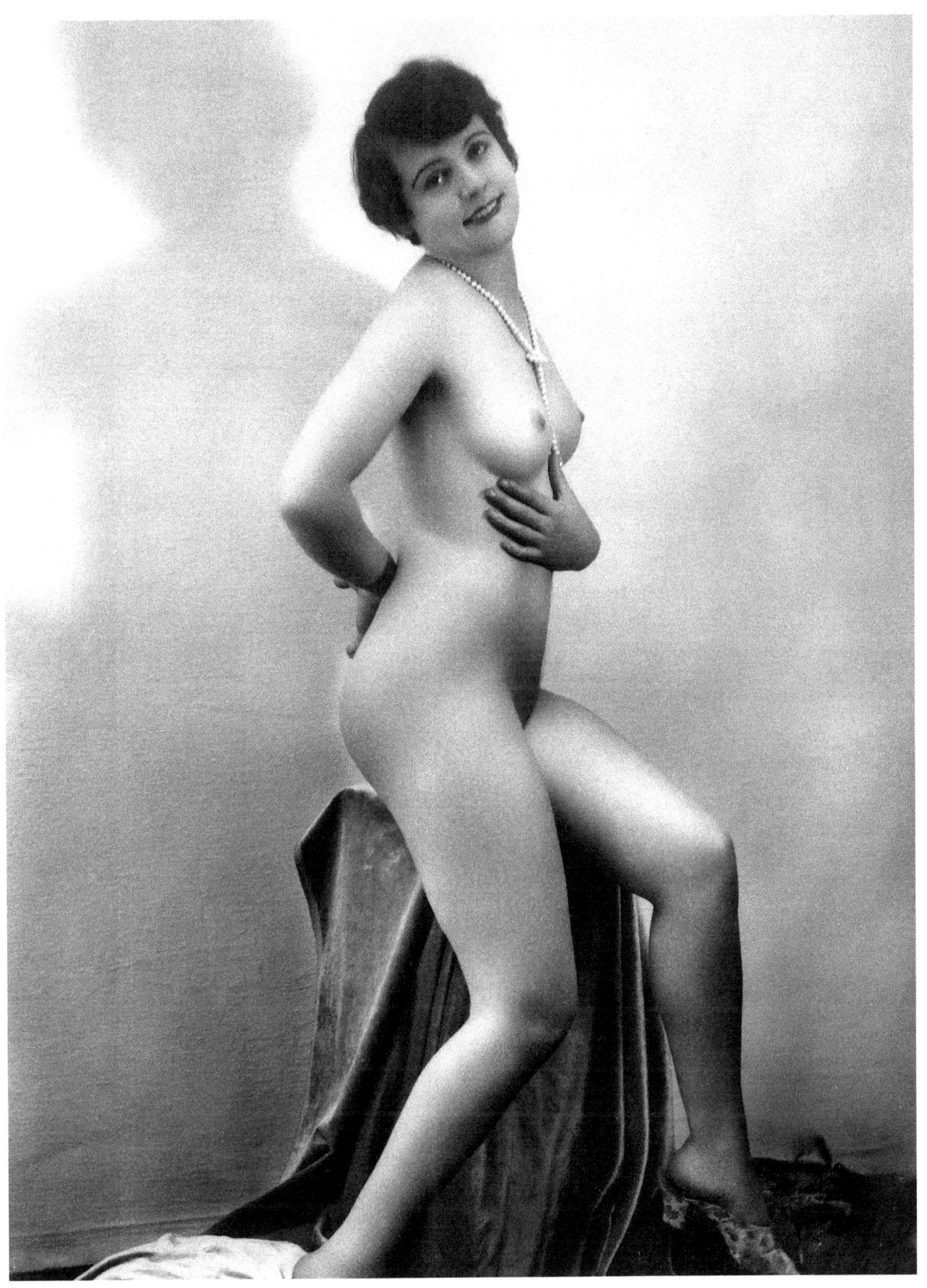

Nude Woman With Pigeons

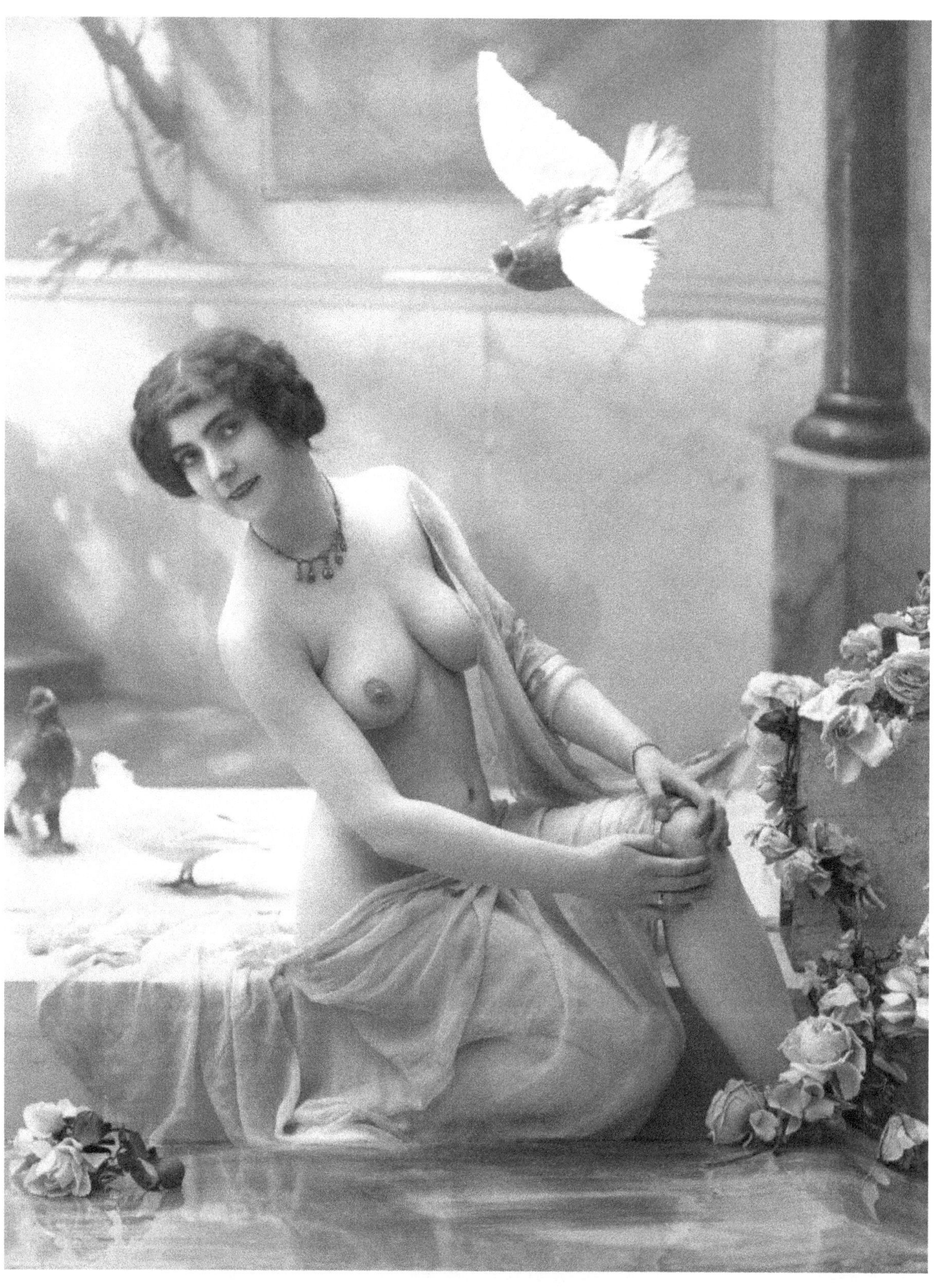

Nude Woman in Upraised Arm Pose

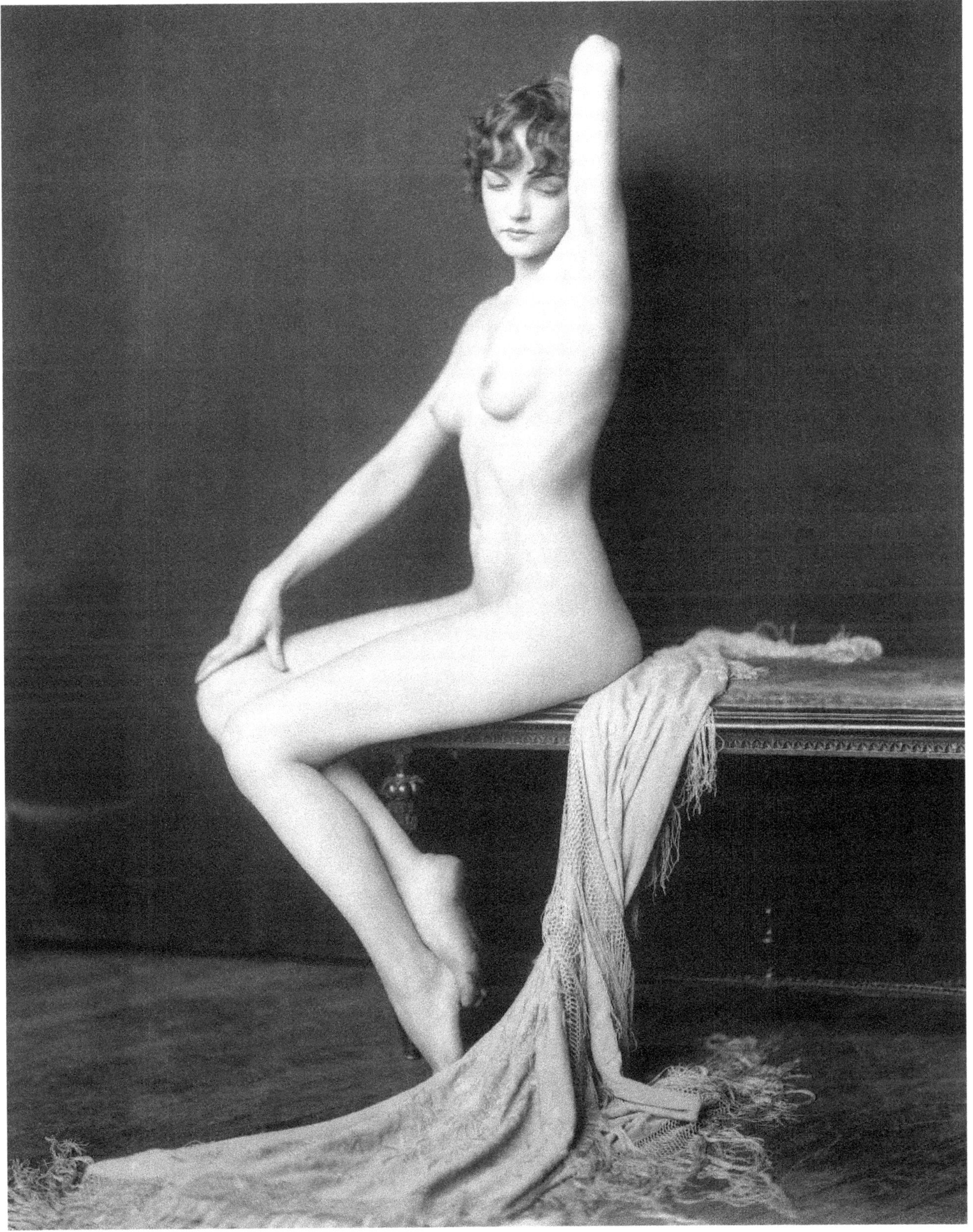

Mata Hari, Exotic Dancer, World War One Spy

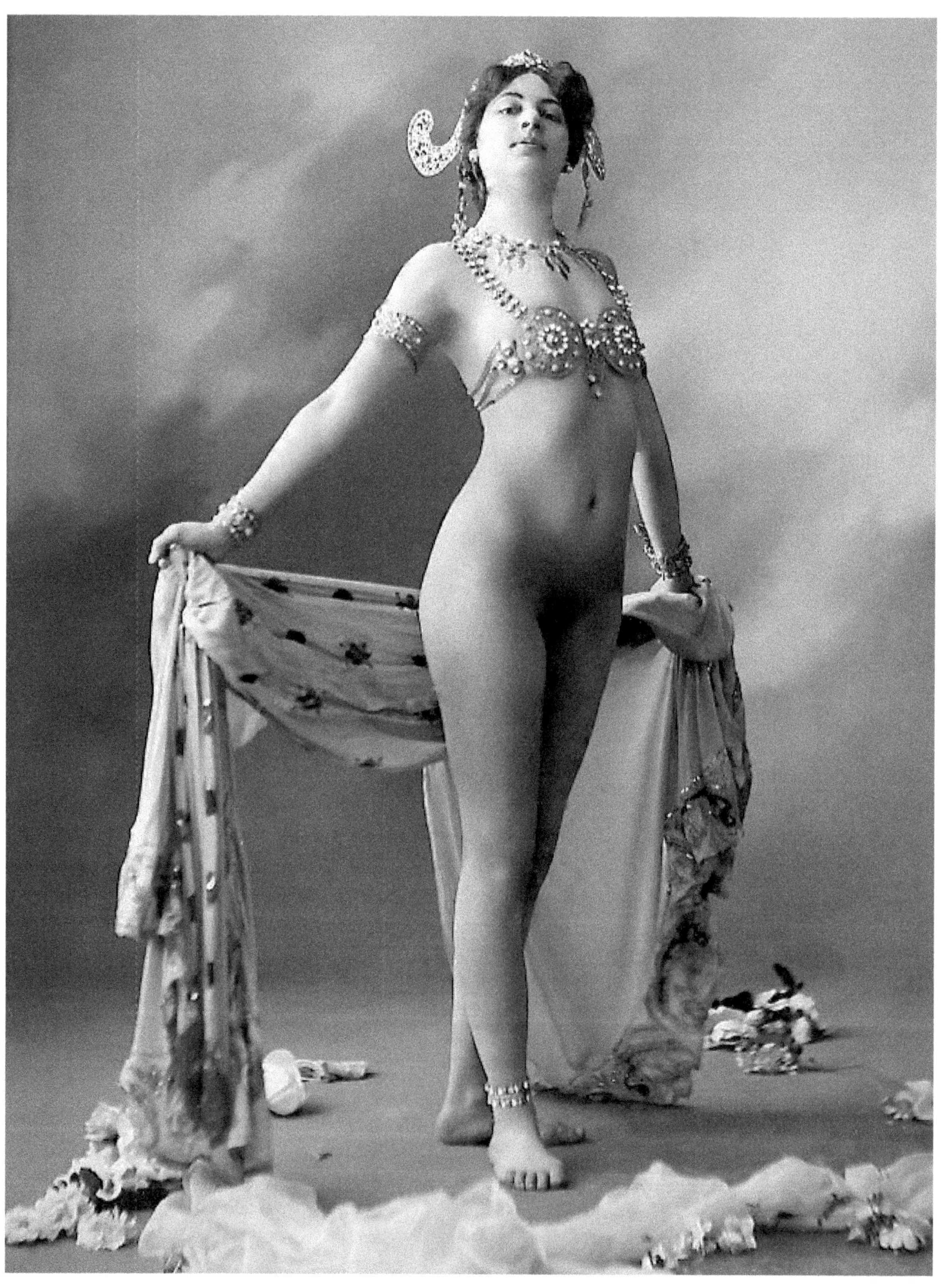

Lovely Nude Woman Sitting On Chair

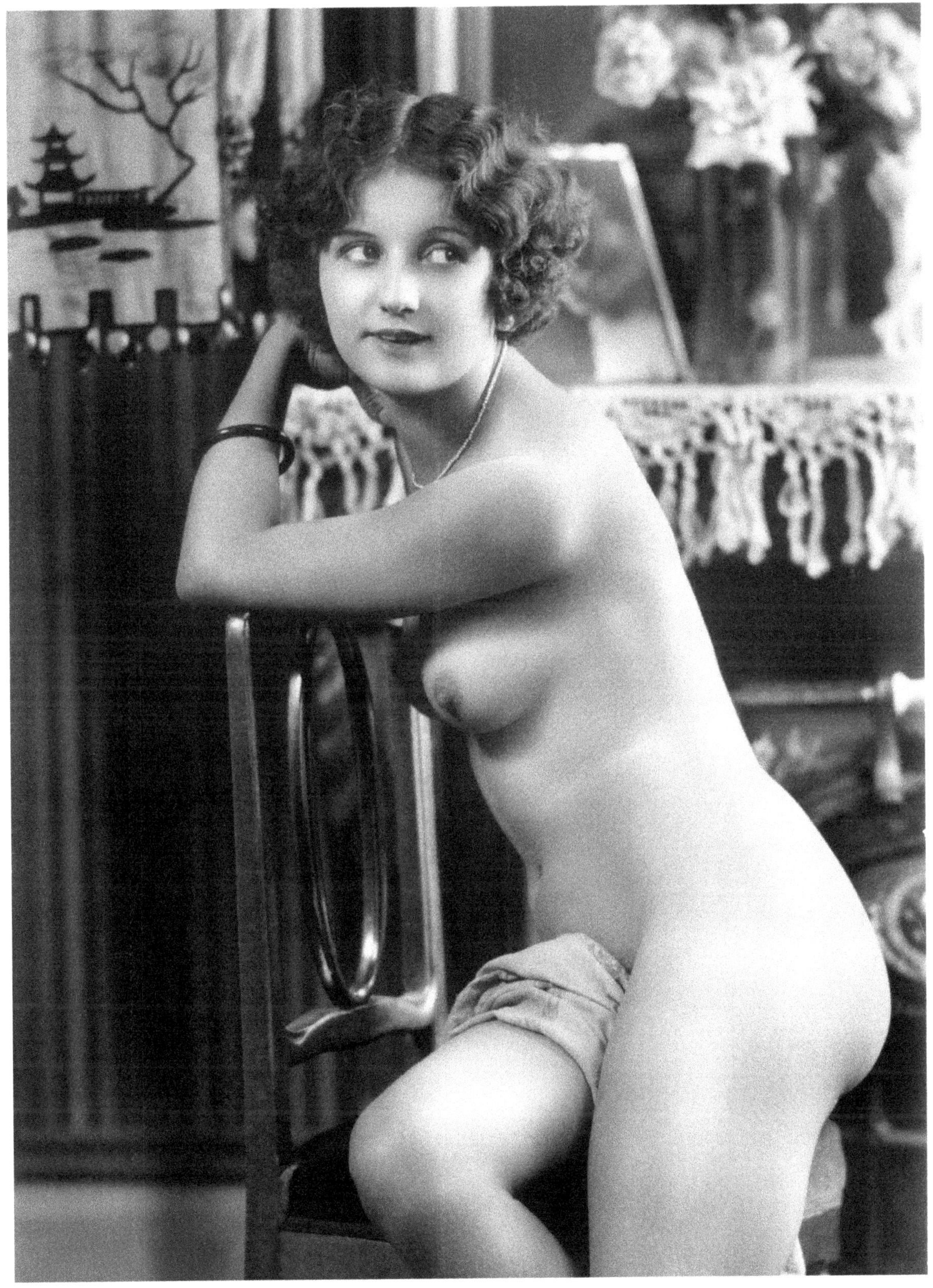

Nude Woman Sitting On Table

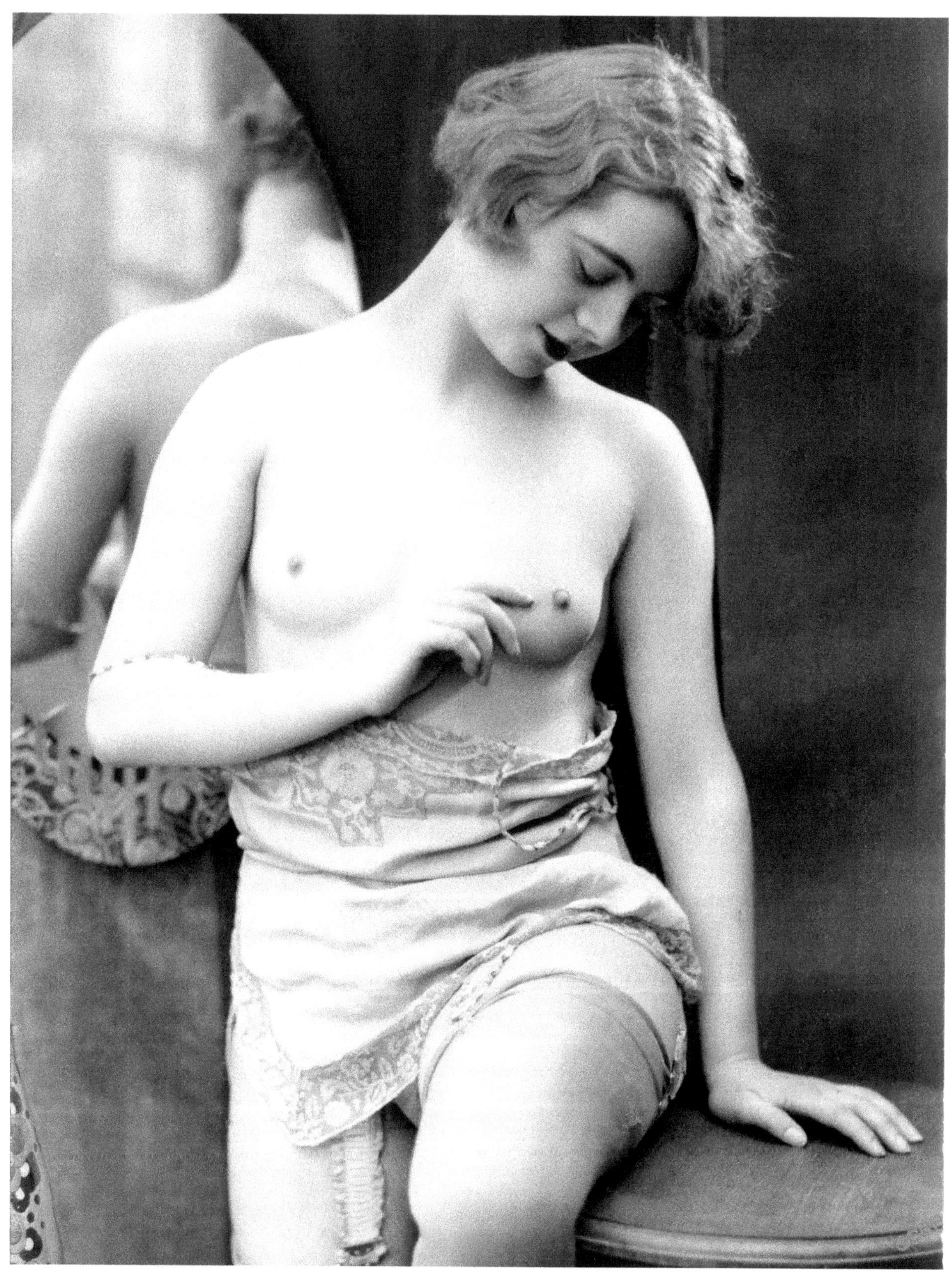

Nude Woman Lounging "French" Postcard

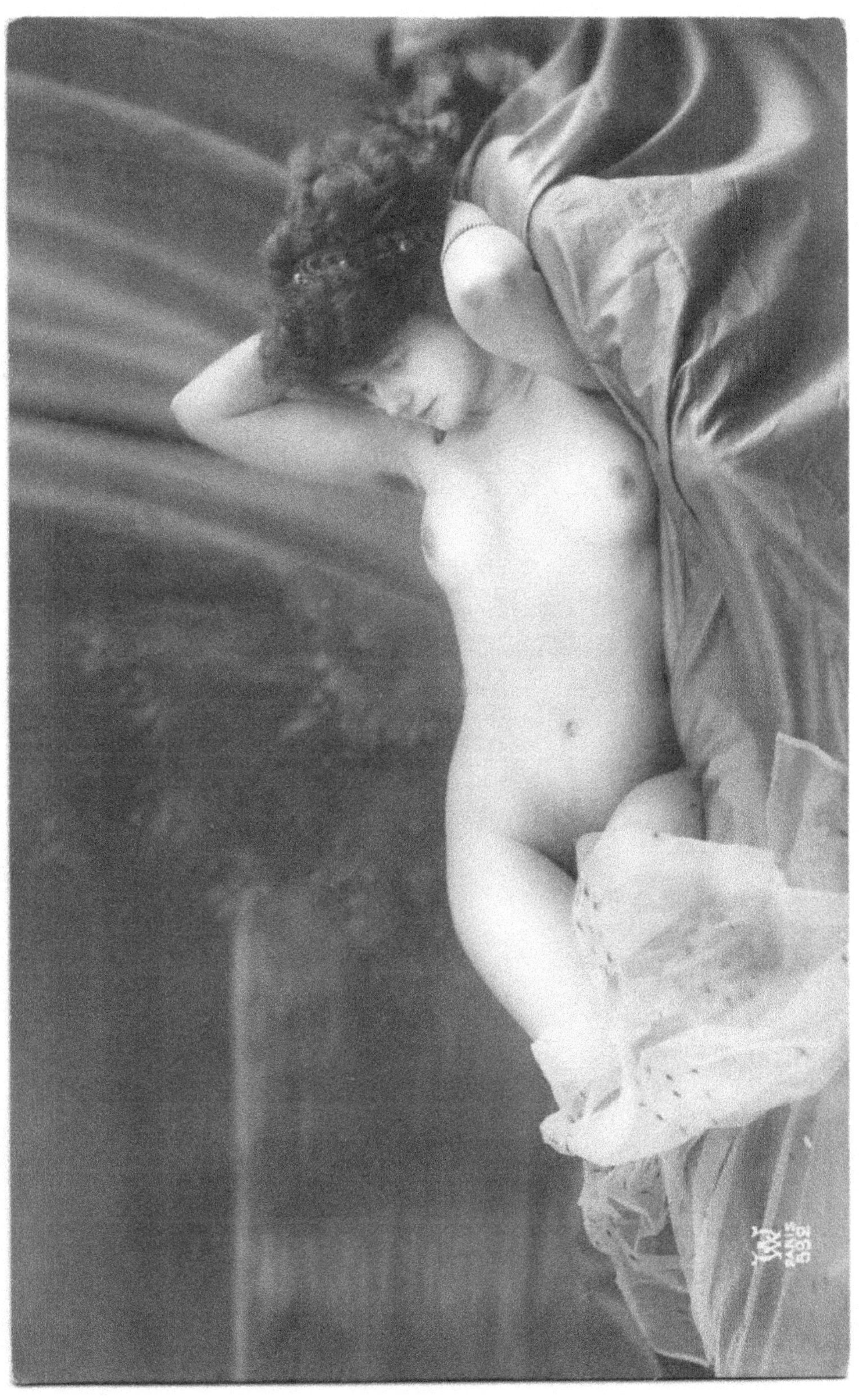

Nude Moroccan Woman Serving Mint Tea

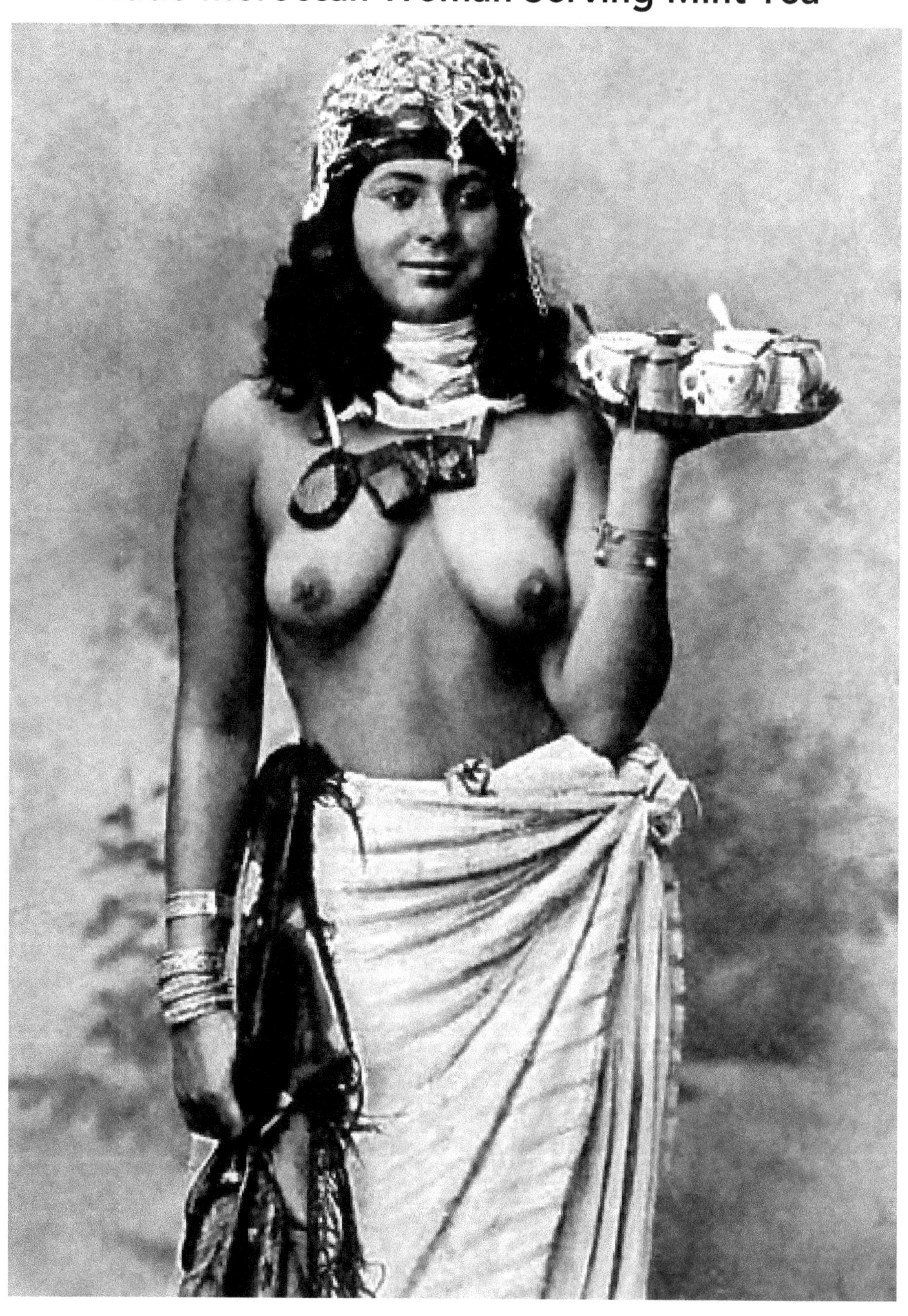

Nude Woman With Pearls Kneeling

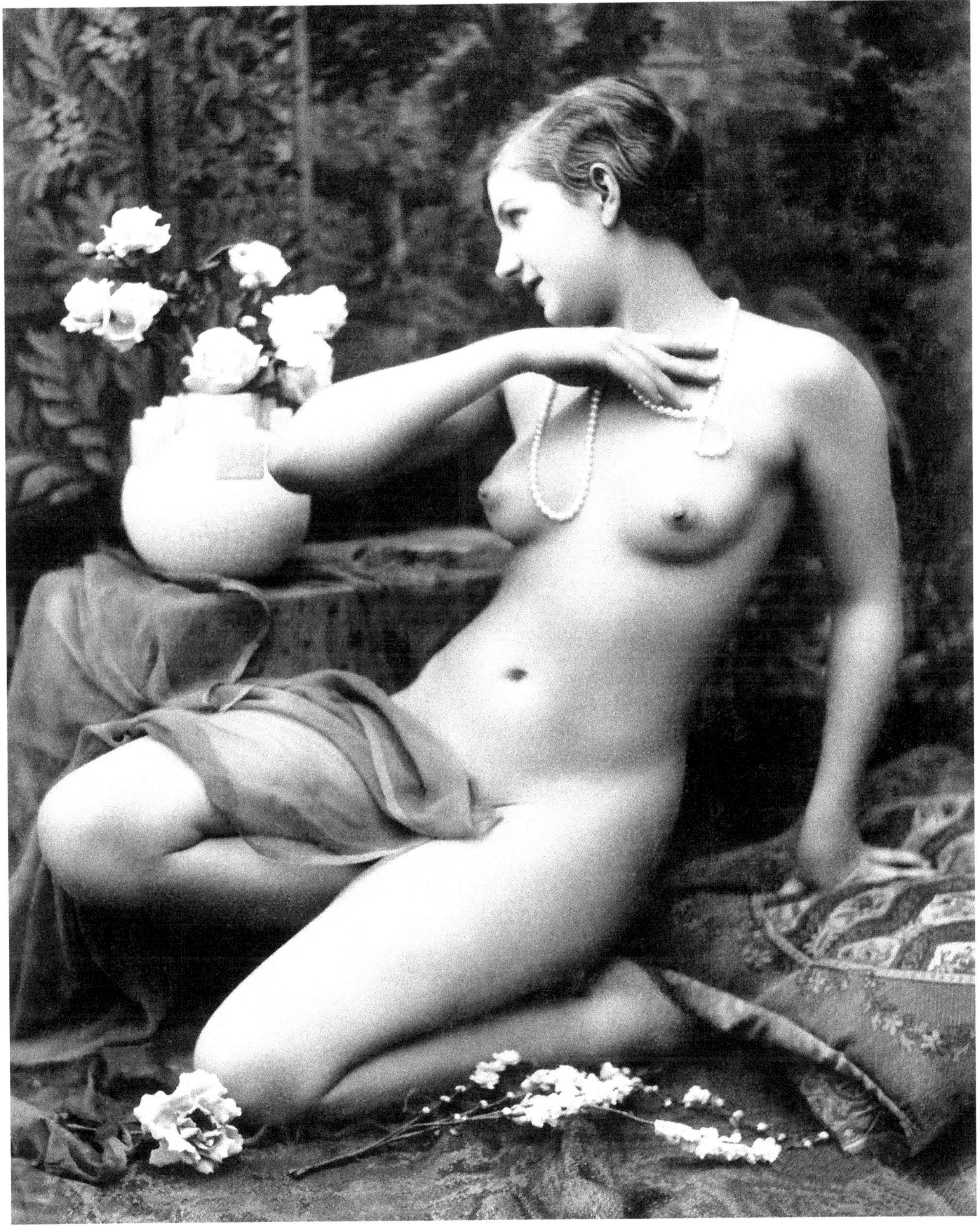

Woman Teasingly Reveals One Breast

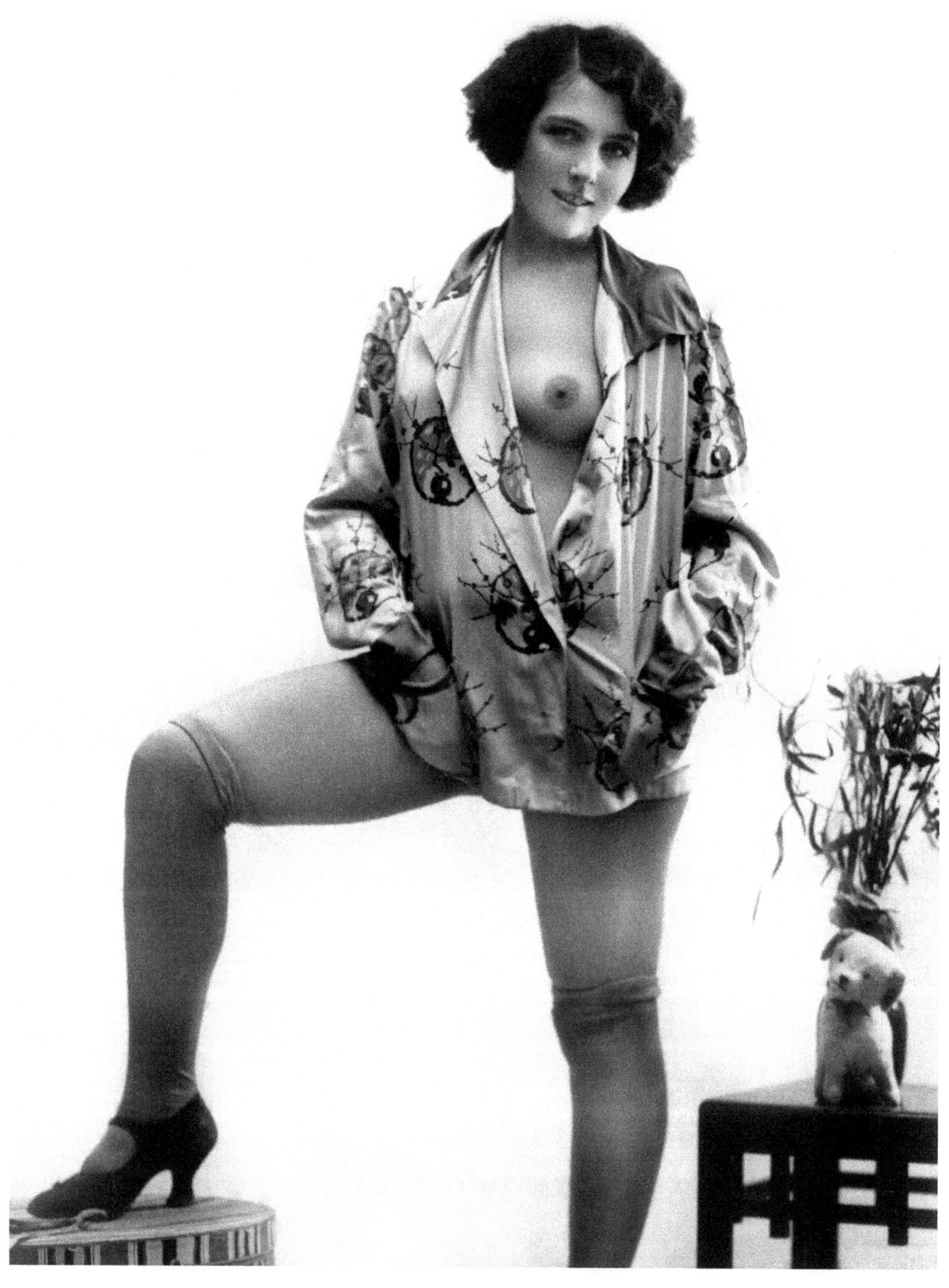

Thin Nude Woman on Stage

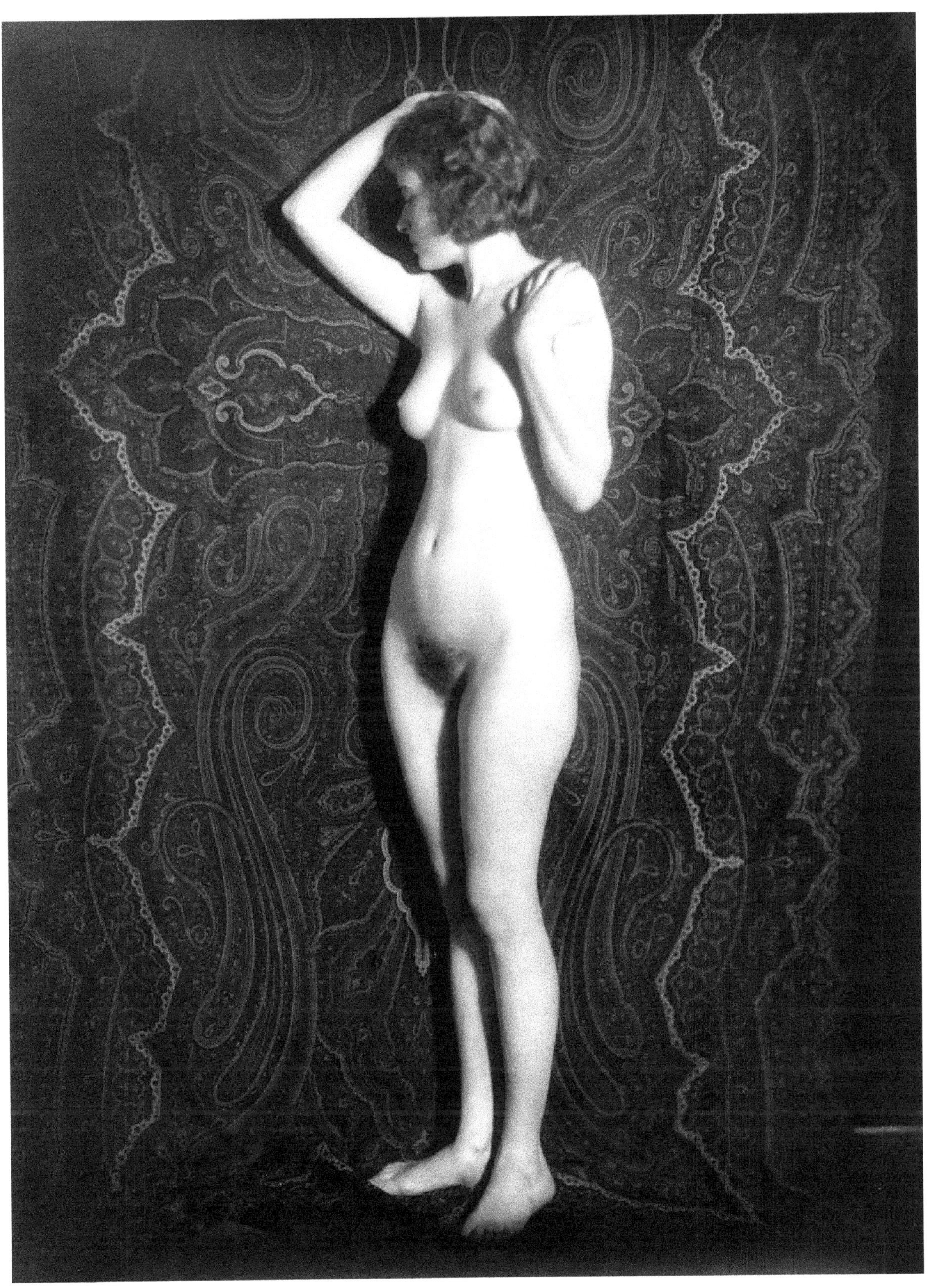

Nude Woman Lounging Wearing Only a String Of Pearls

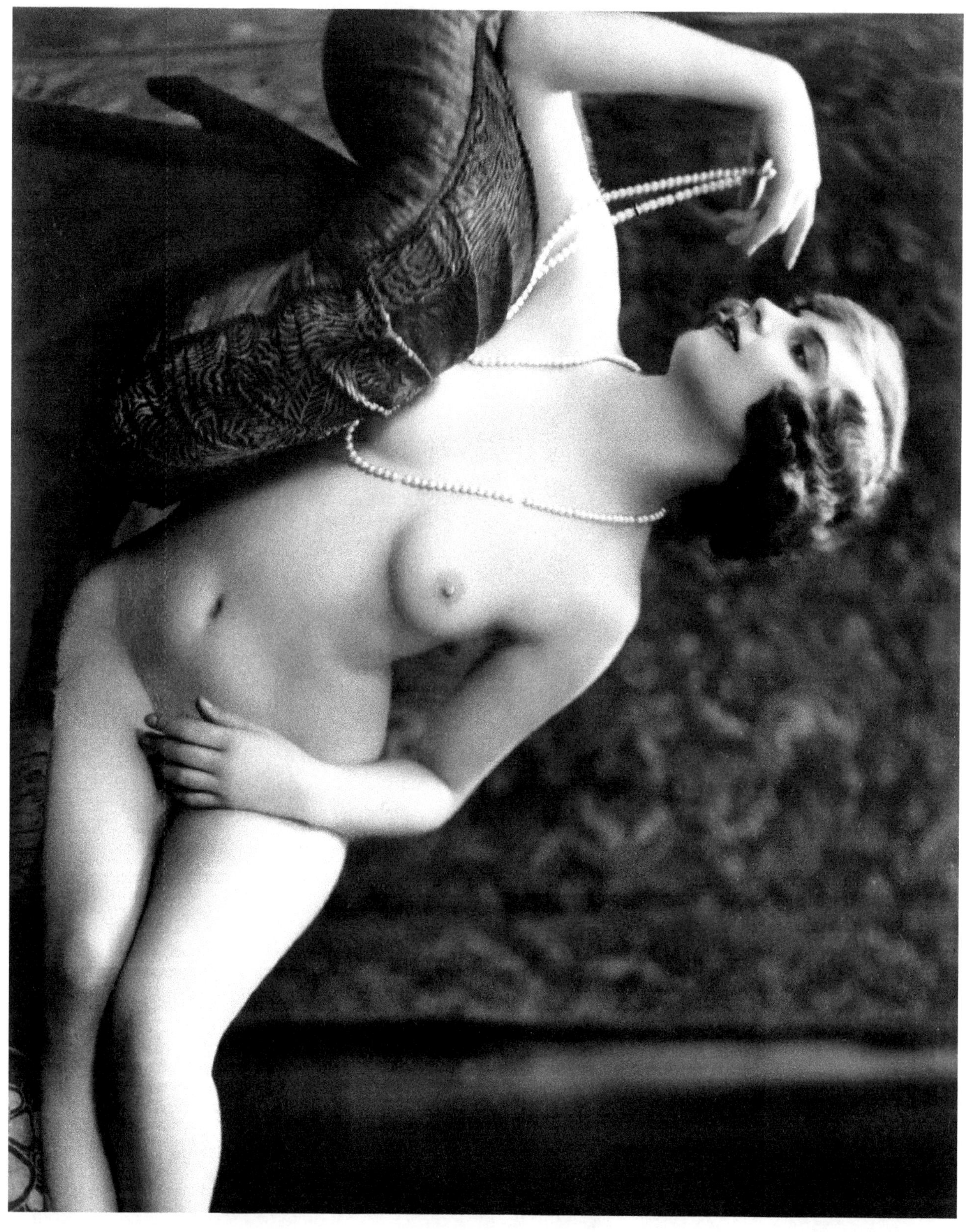

Nude Woman Putting On Pearls

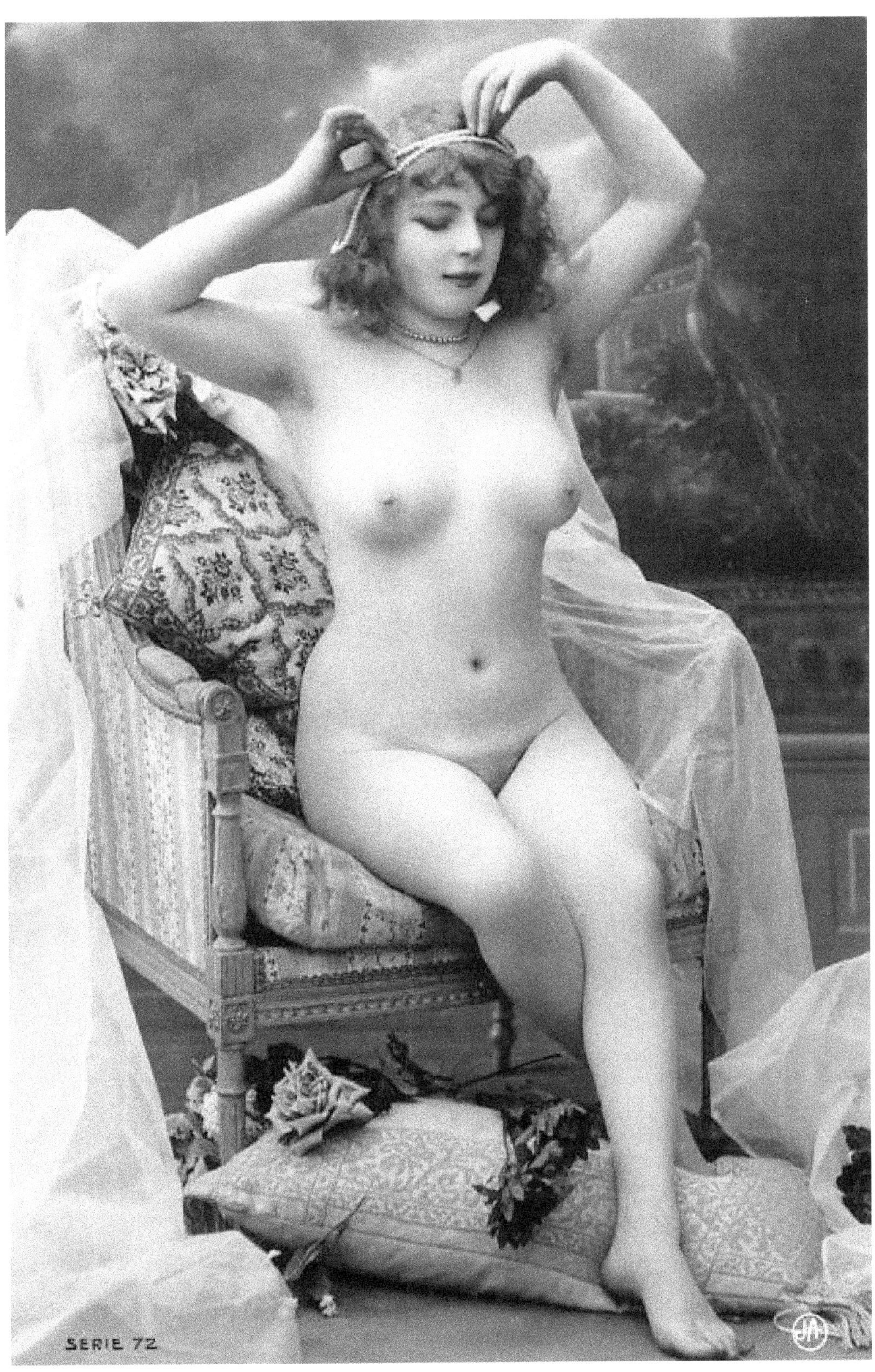

Nude Woman Wearing Costume Jewelry

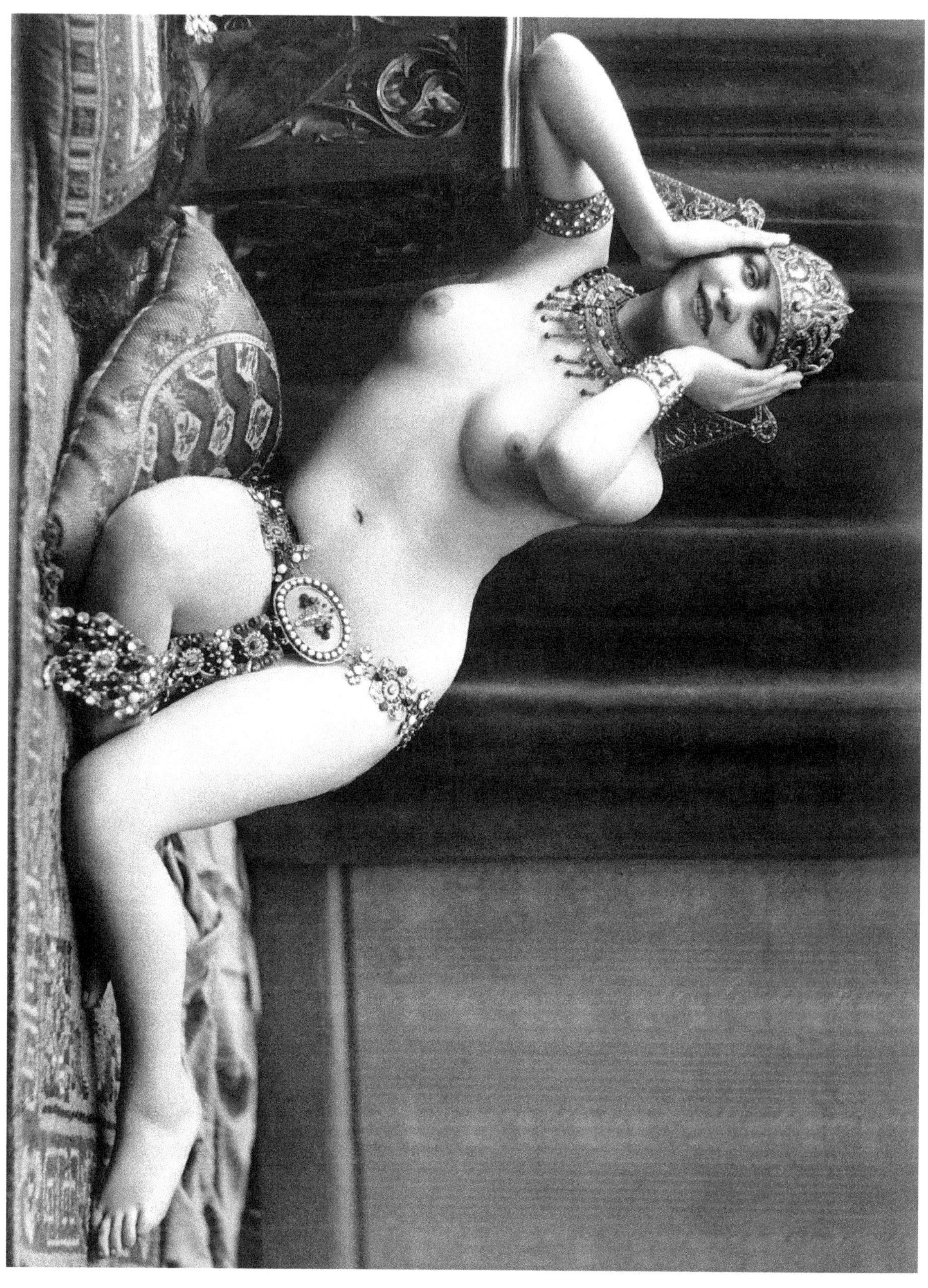

Nude Woman Acting Coy

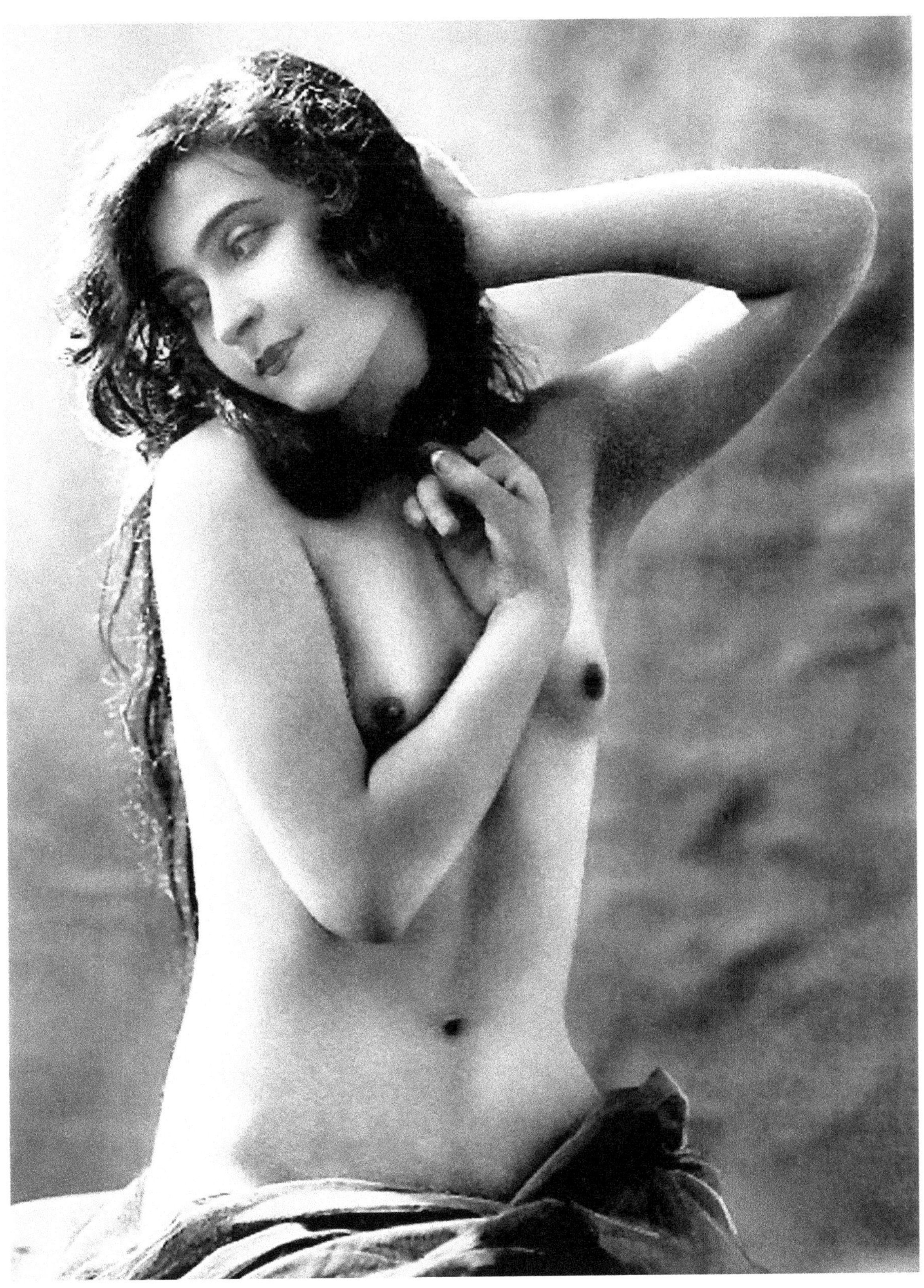

Nude Woman On Vanity Reflected in Mirror

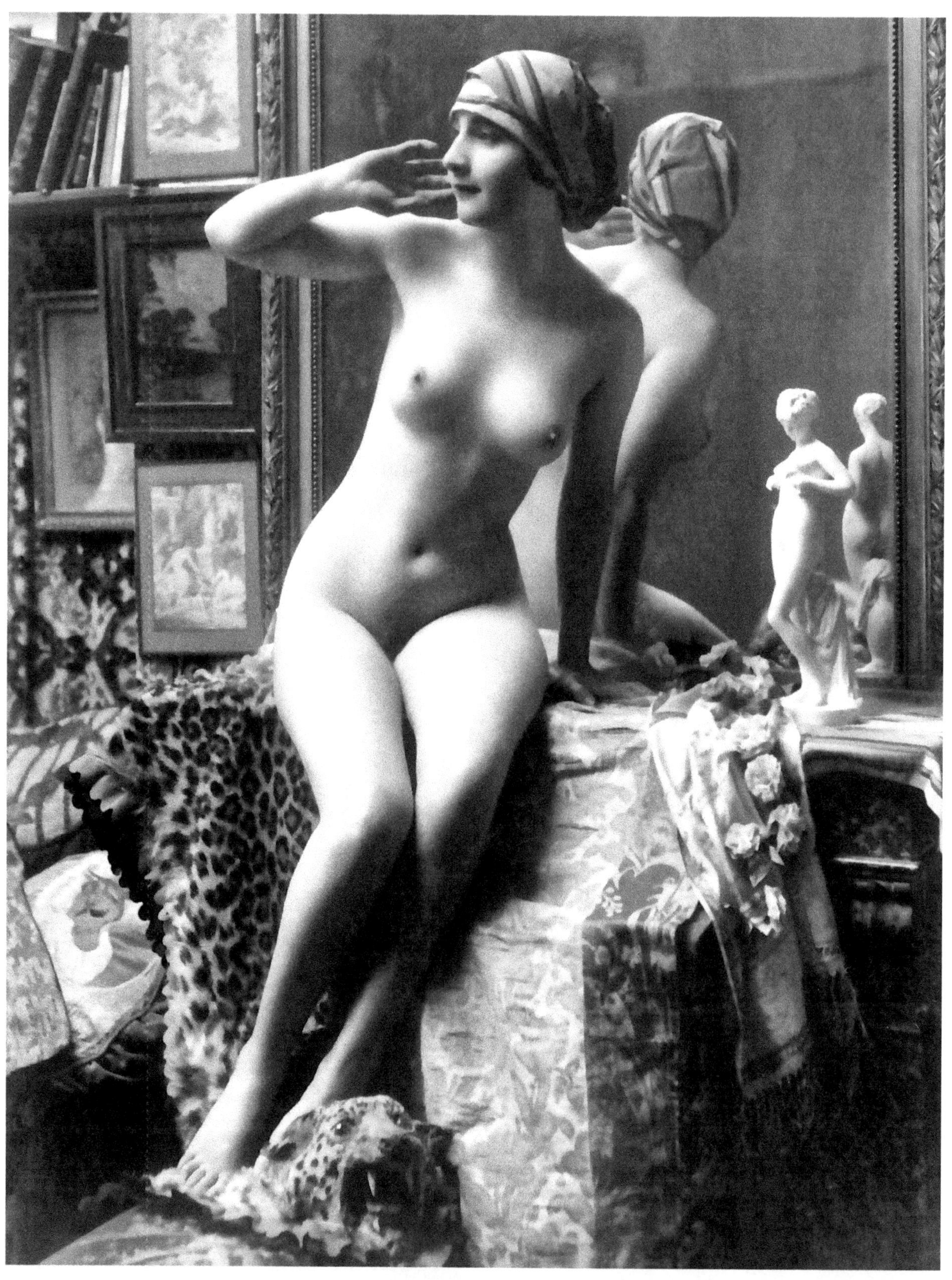

Nude Woman Sits Comfortably in Chair

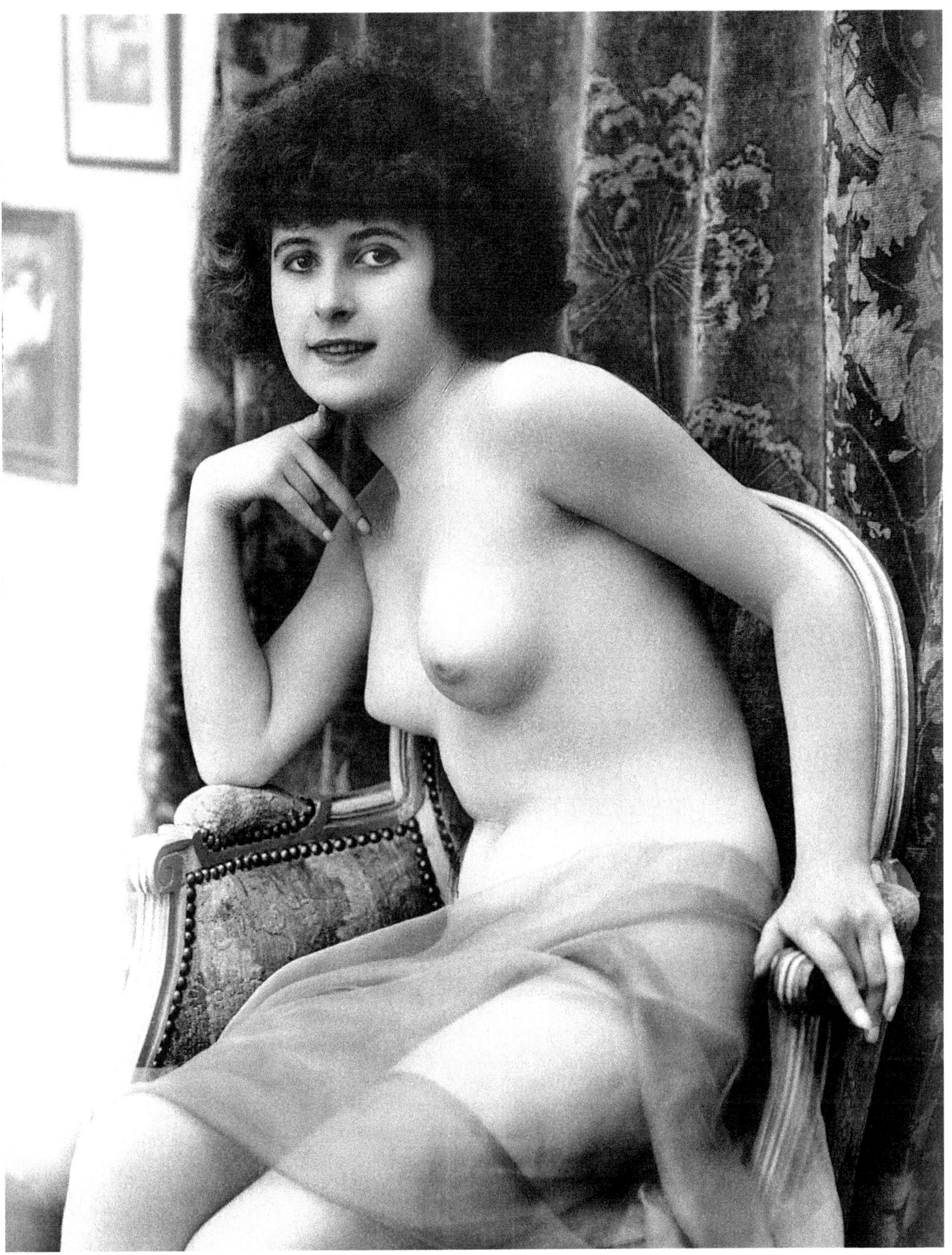

Nude Woman With Puppet

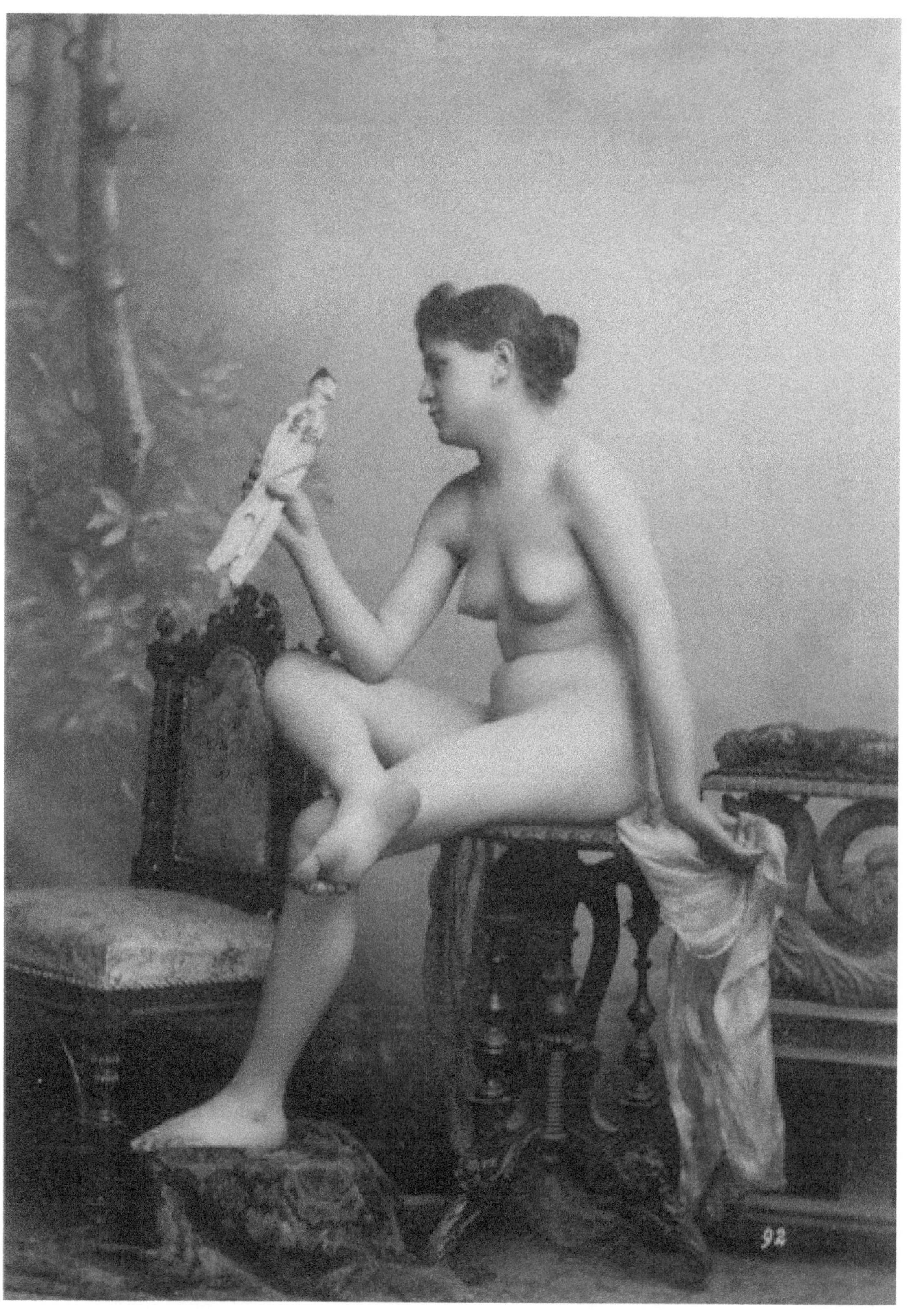

Nude Woman Looks At Reflection

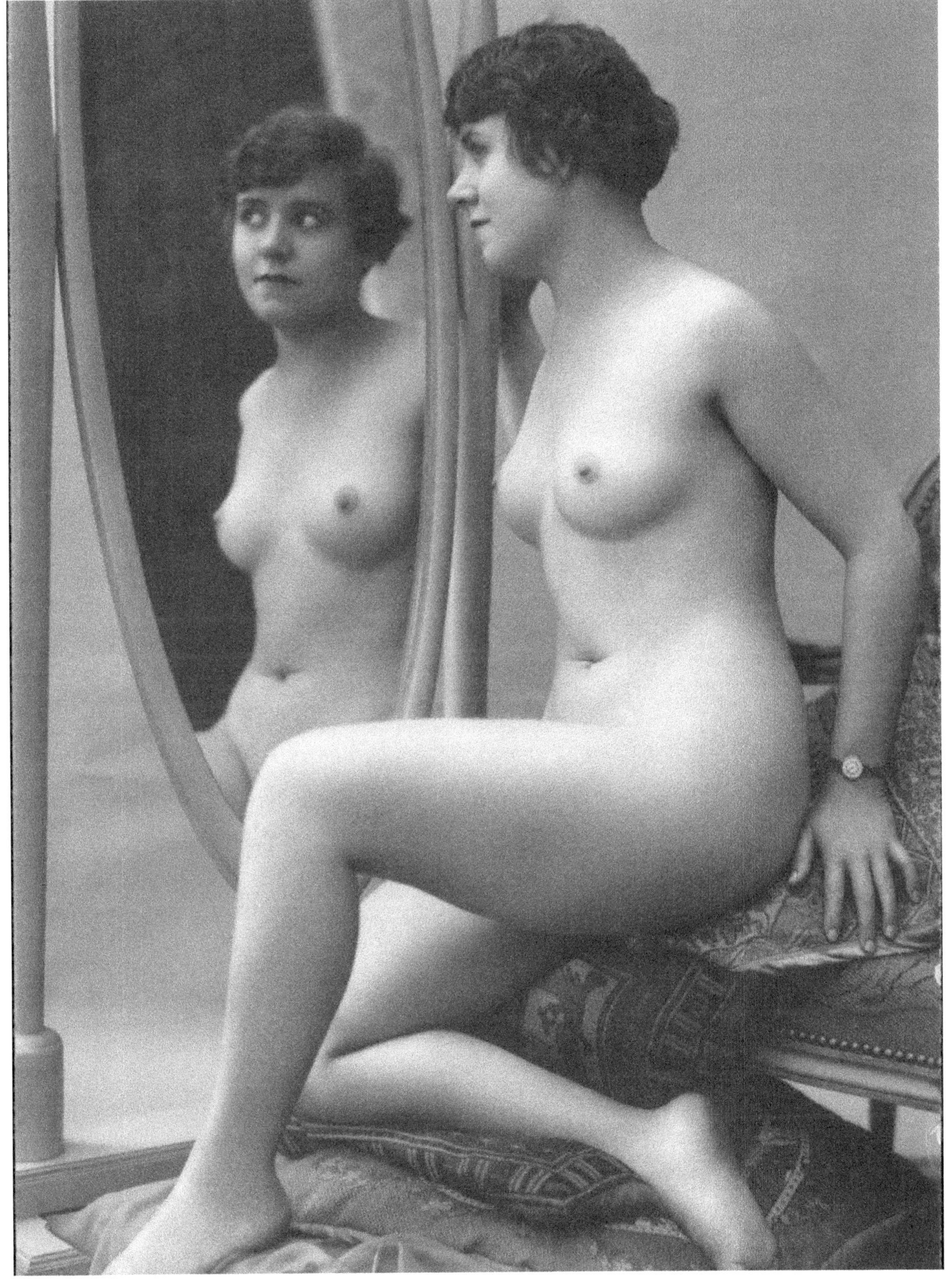

Nude Woman Holds a Rose

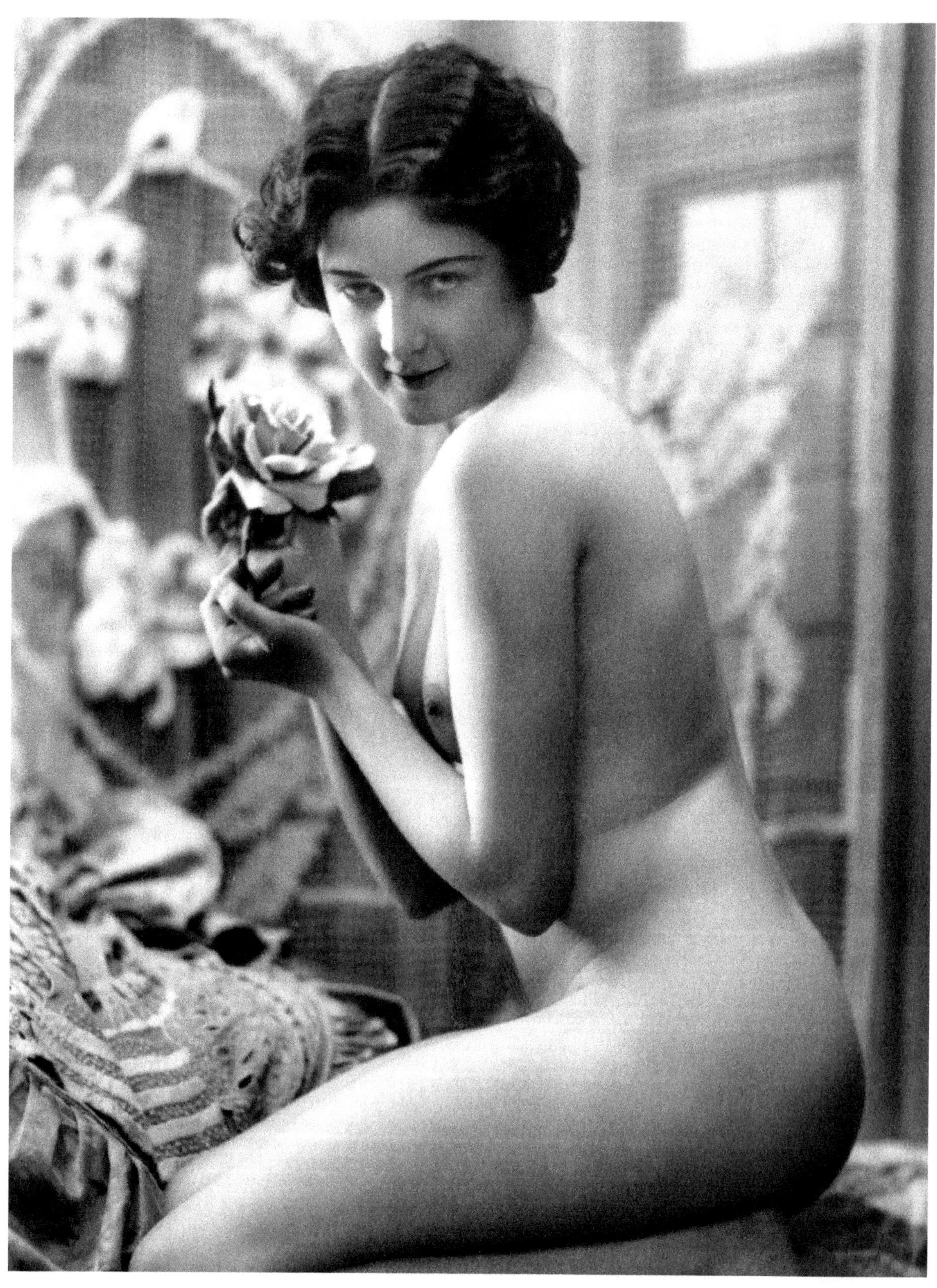

Long Haired Nude Woman With Arm Raised

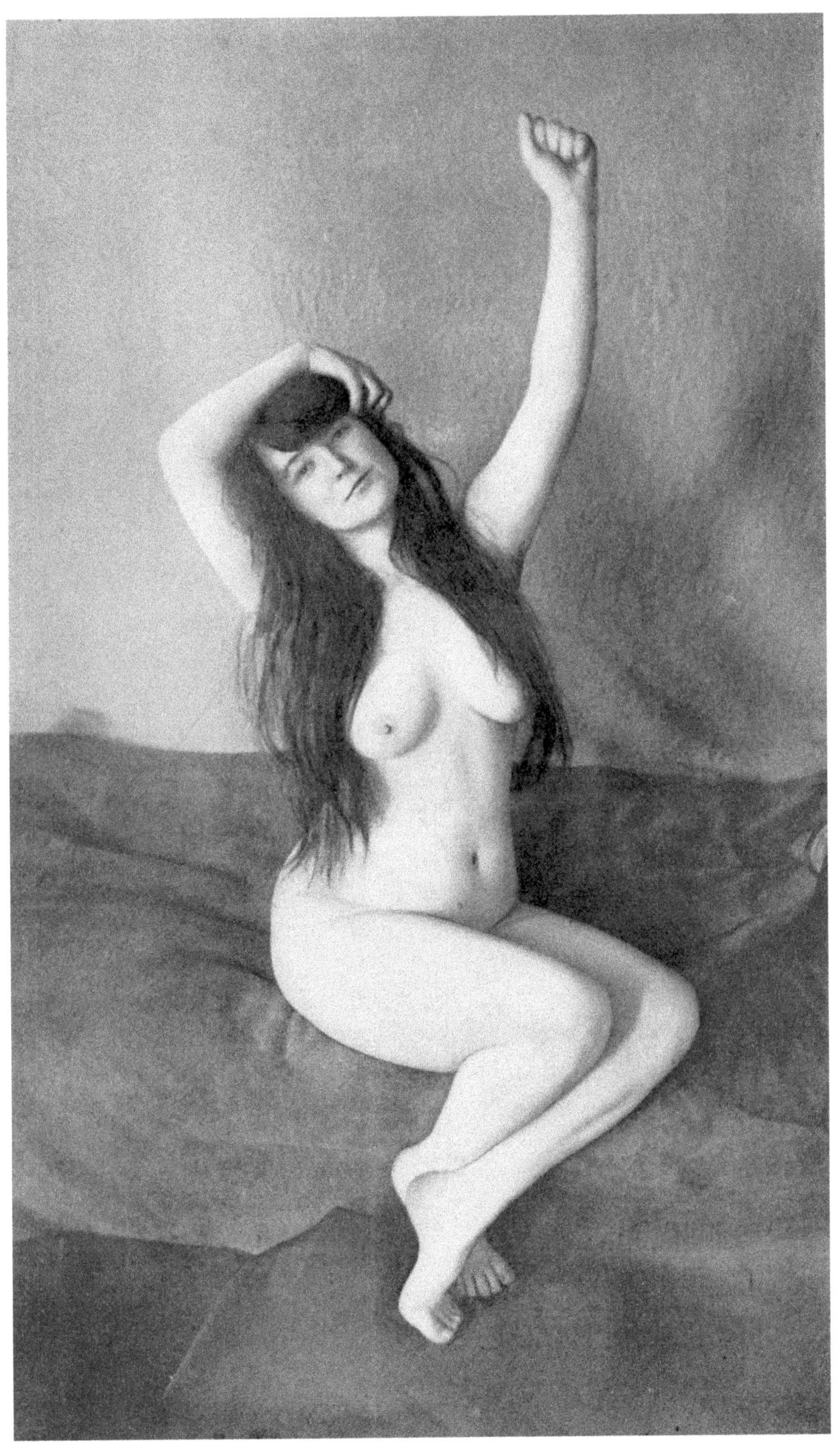

Nude Woman Holding Breast in Bed

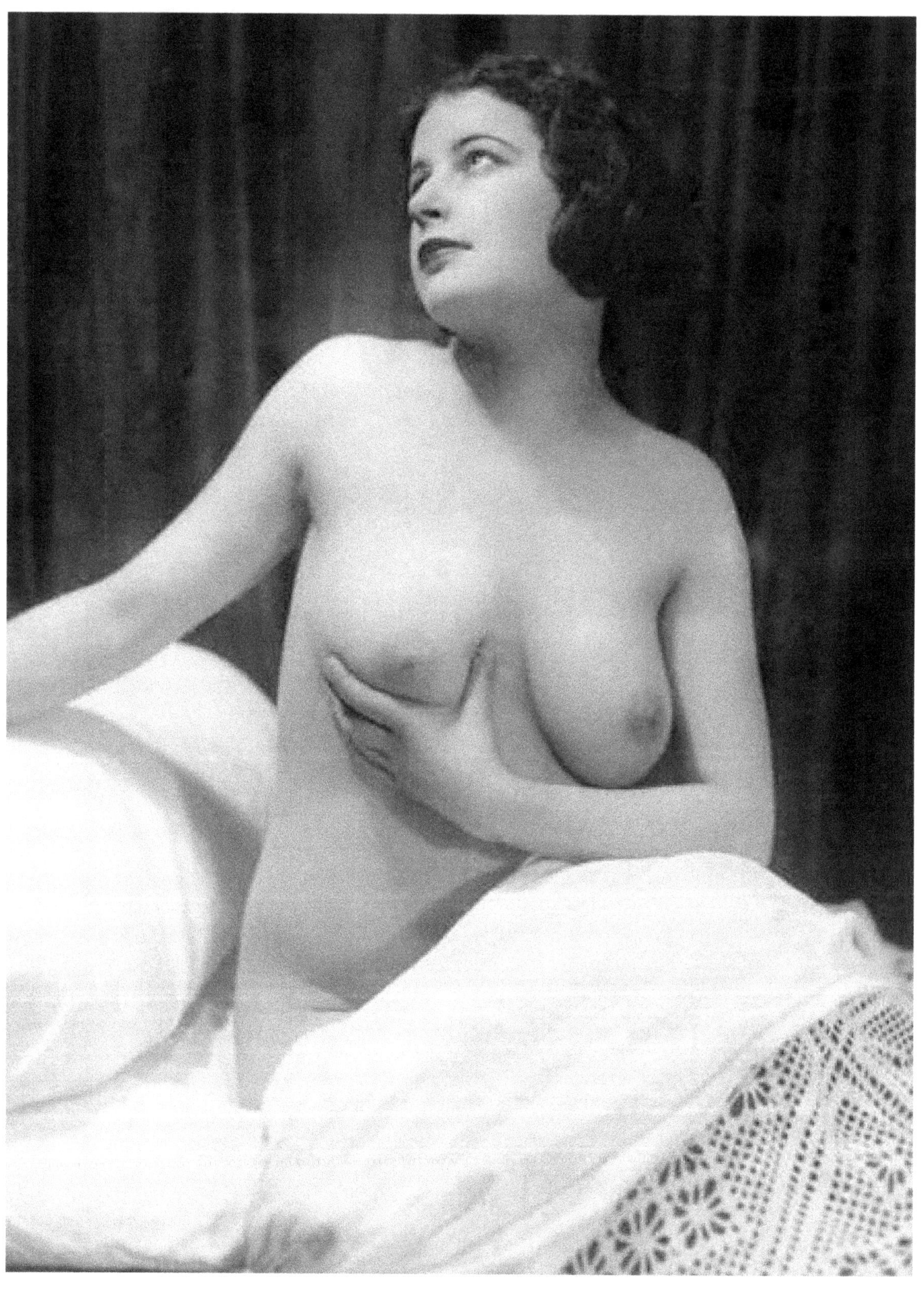

Nude Woman Getting Water

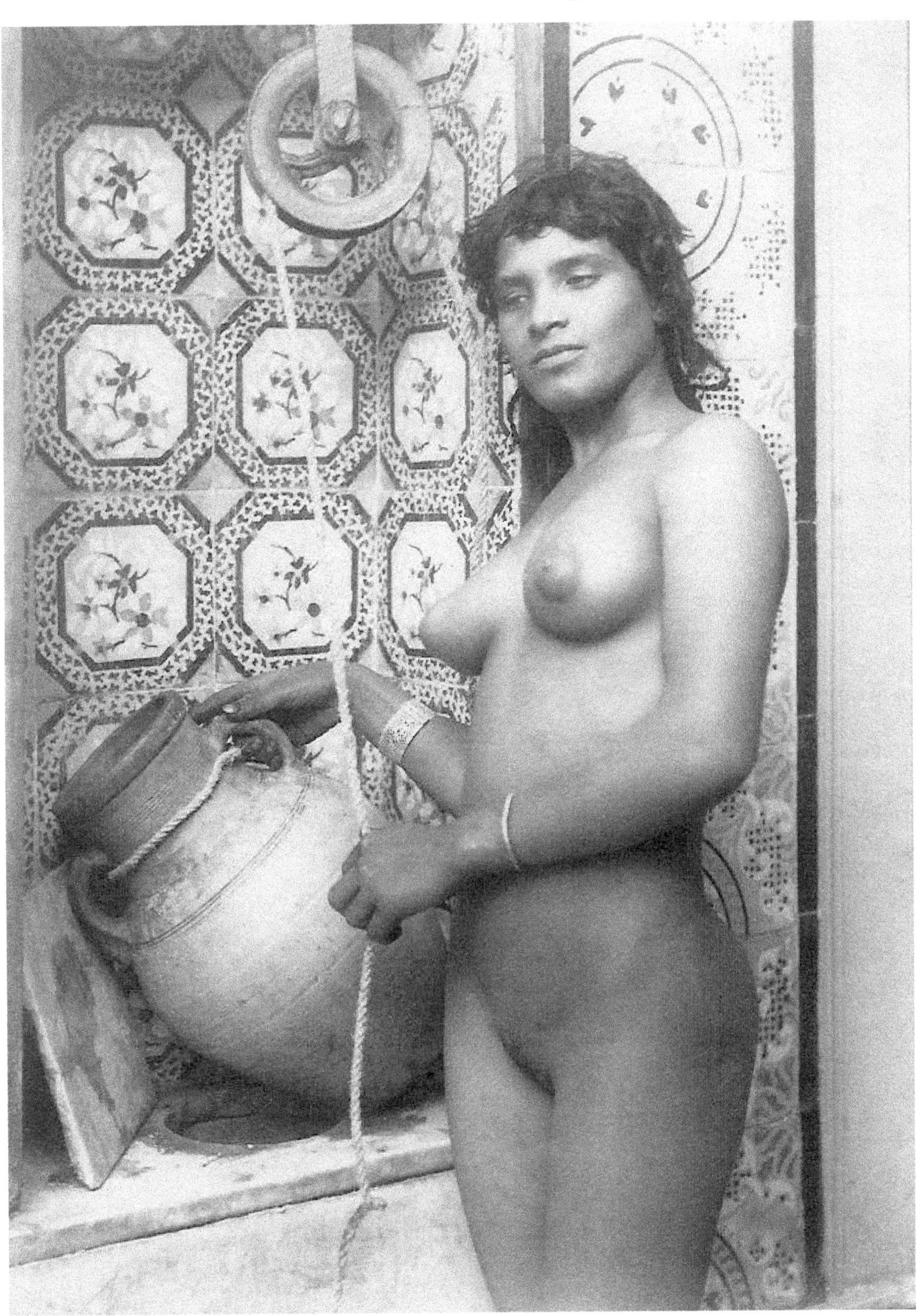

Nude Woman In The Corner

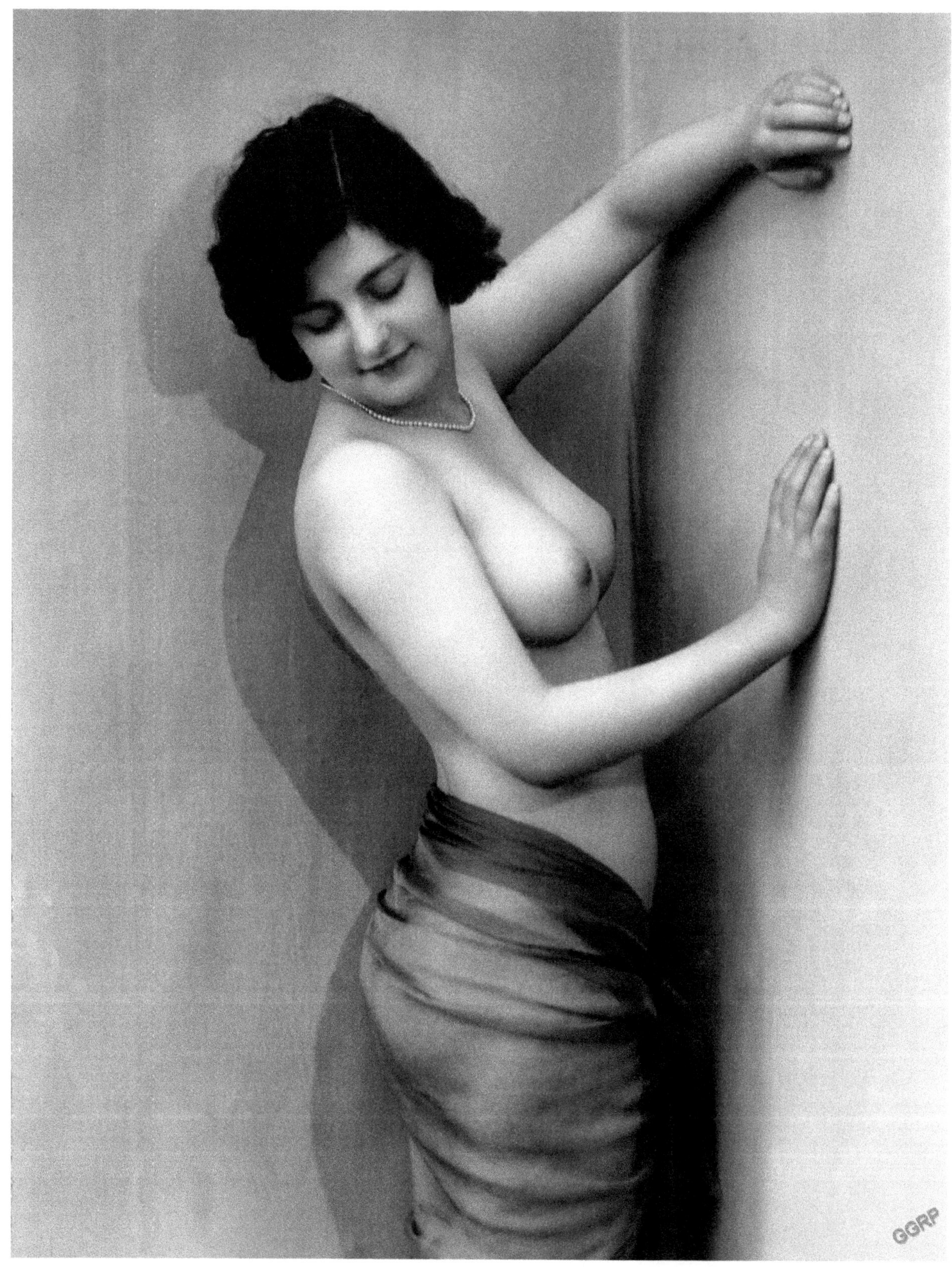

Nude Woman Bares Her Breasts

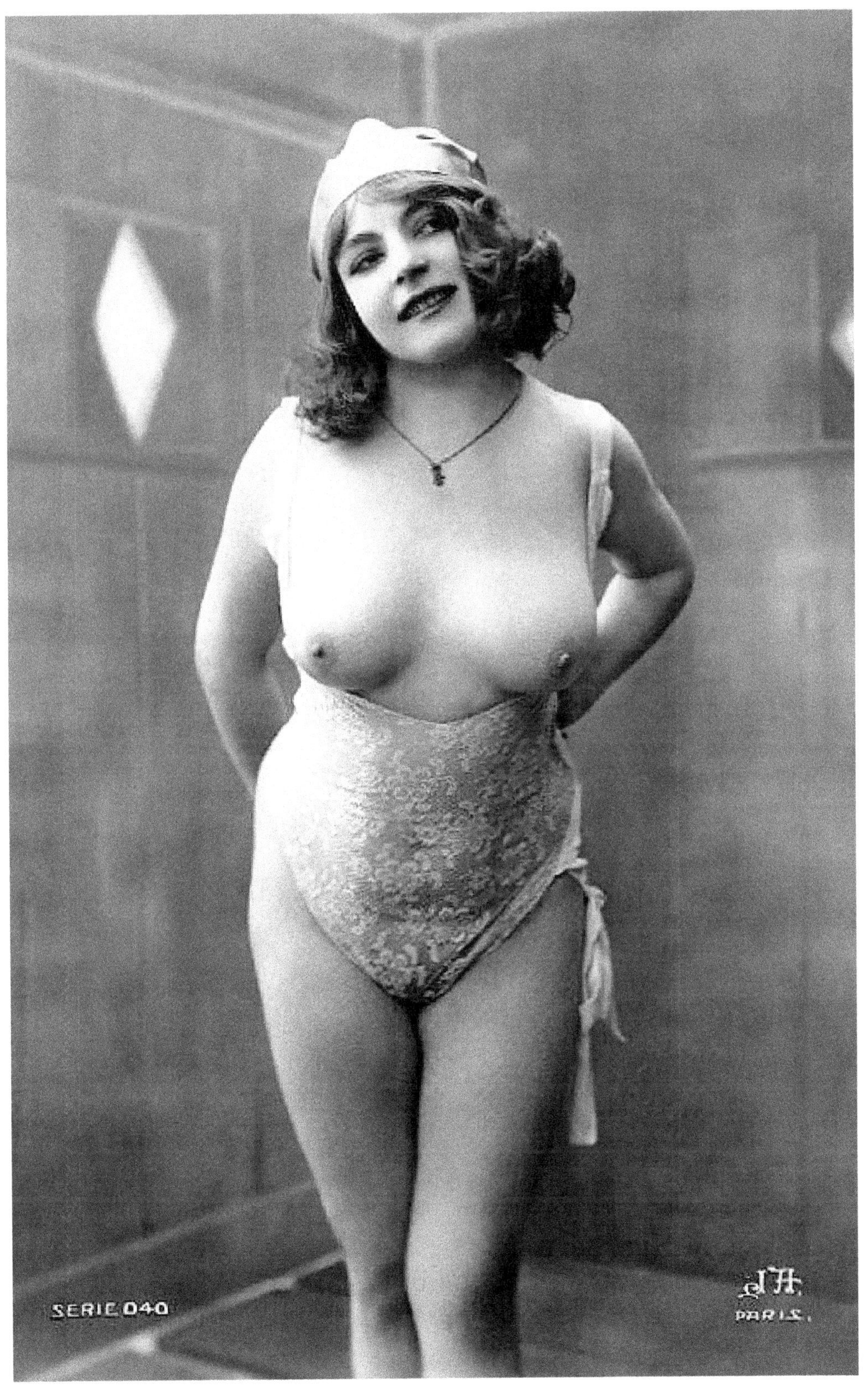

Nude Woman Sitting On a Wall

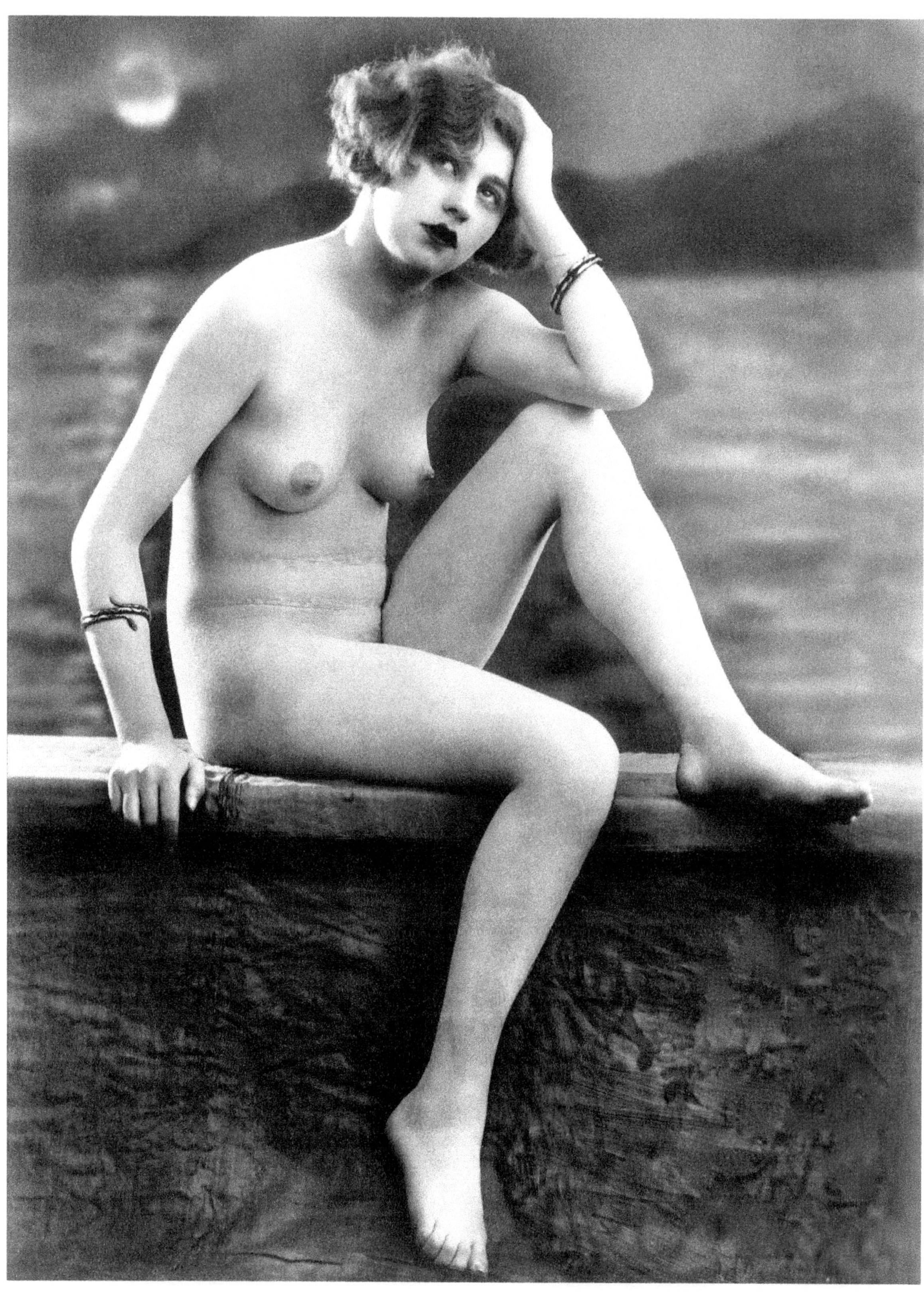

Nude Black Woman in Studio

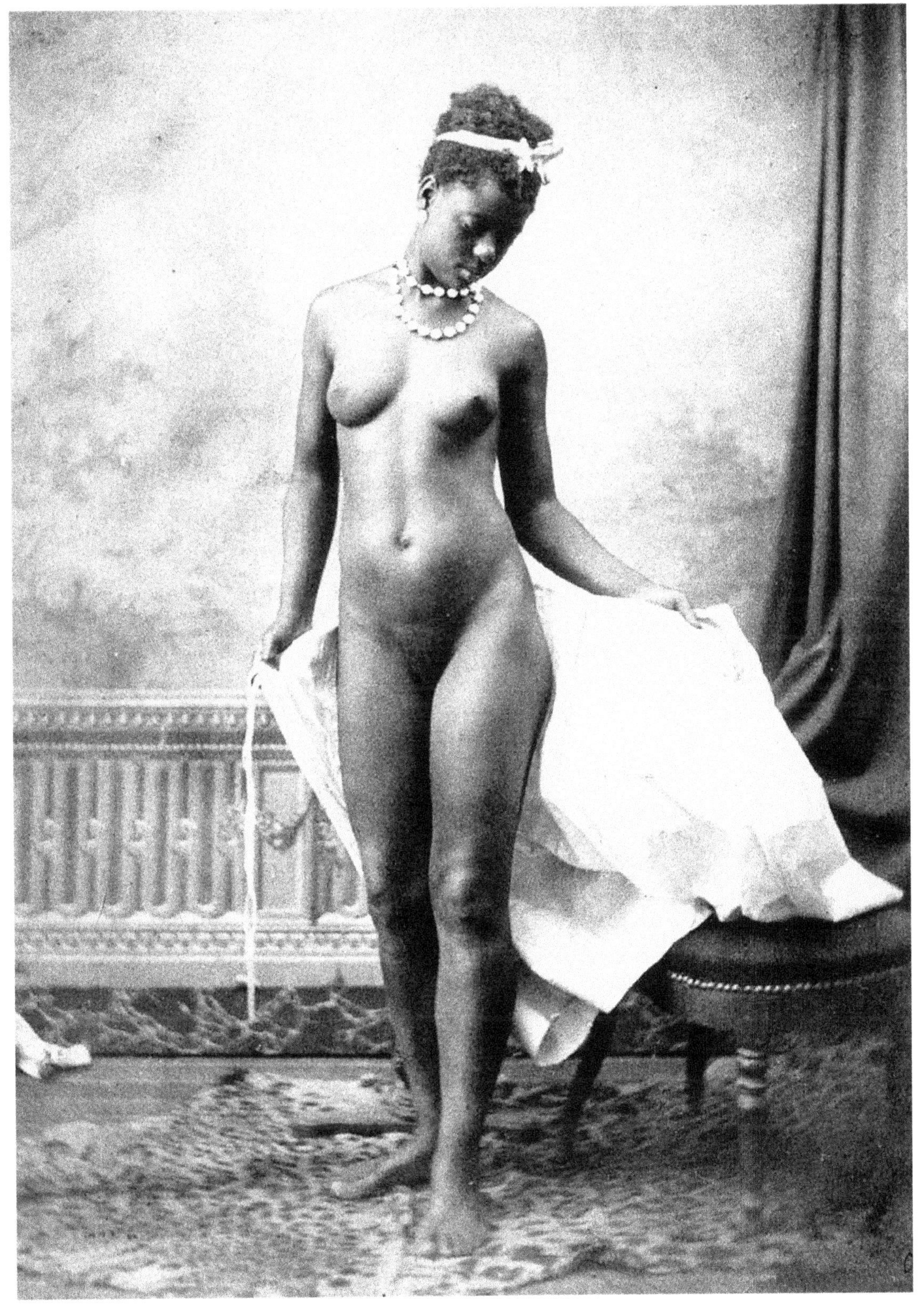

Nude Woman with Friend and Musical Instrument

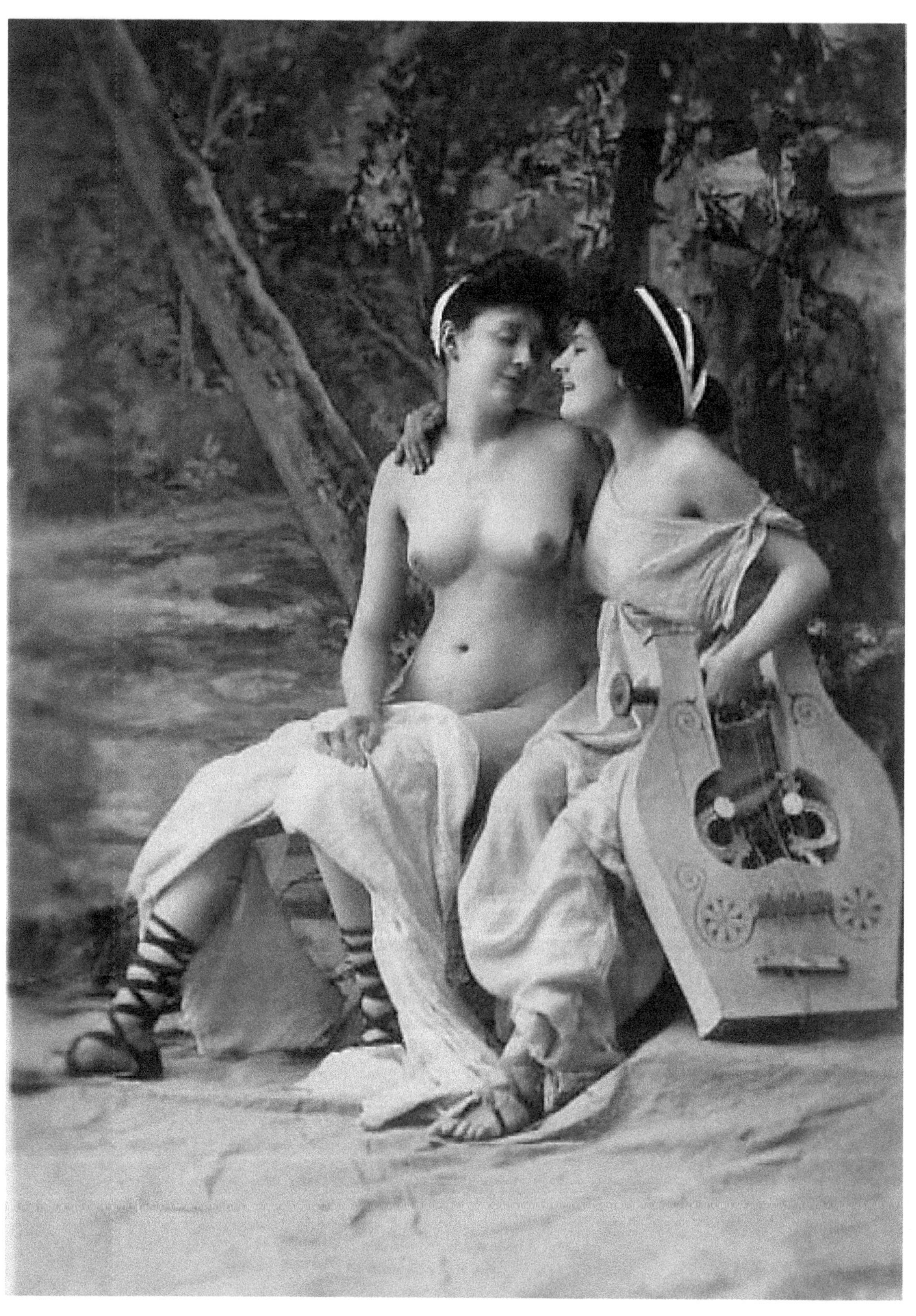

Nude Woman With Pearls Standing

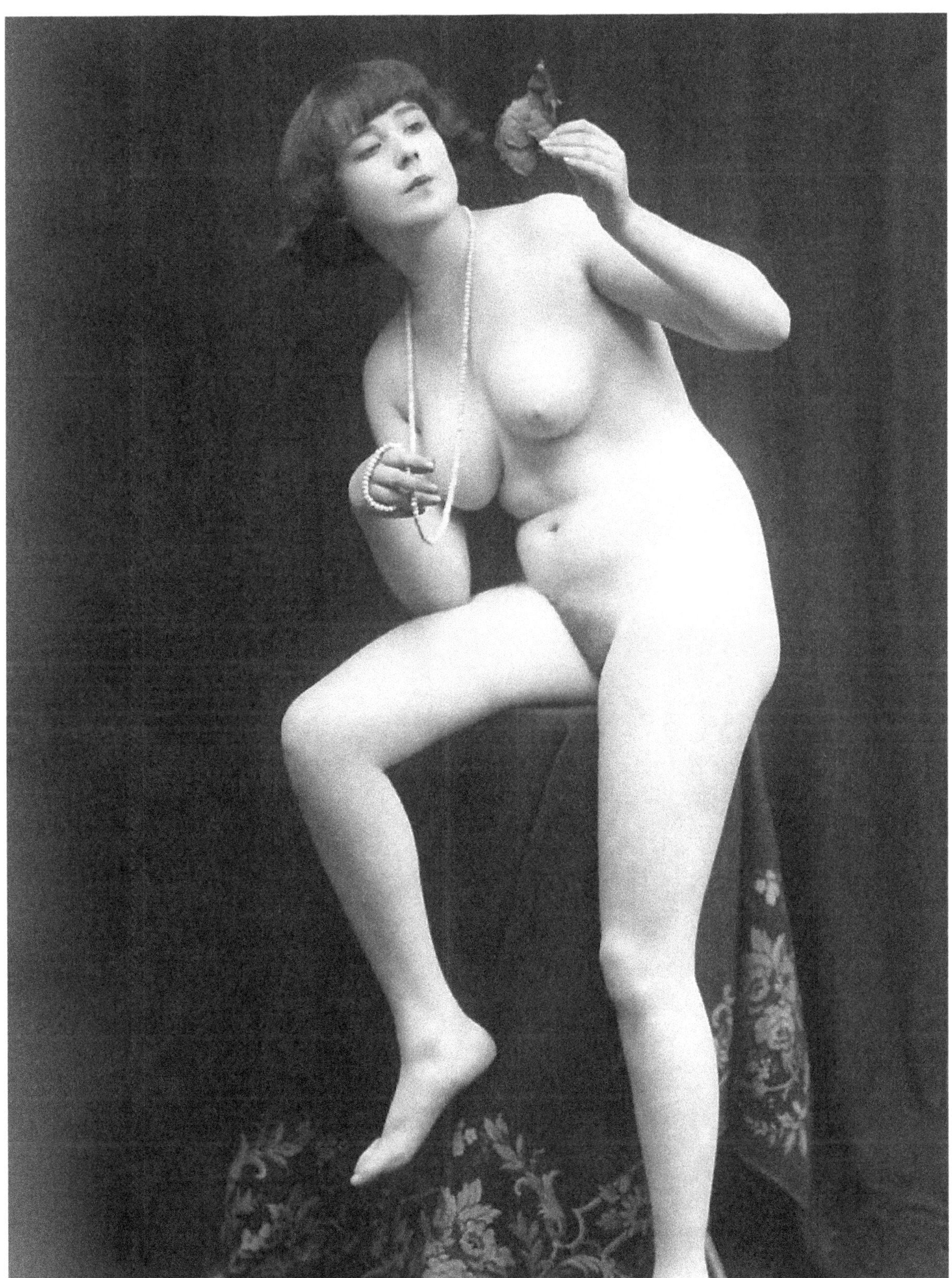

Happy Nude Woman Slightly Draped

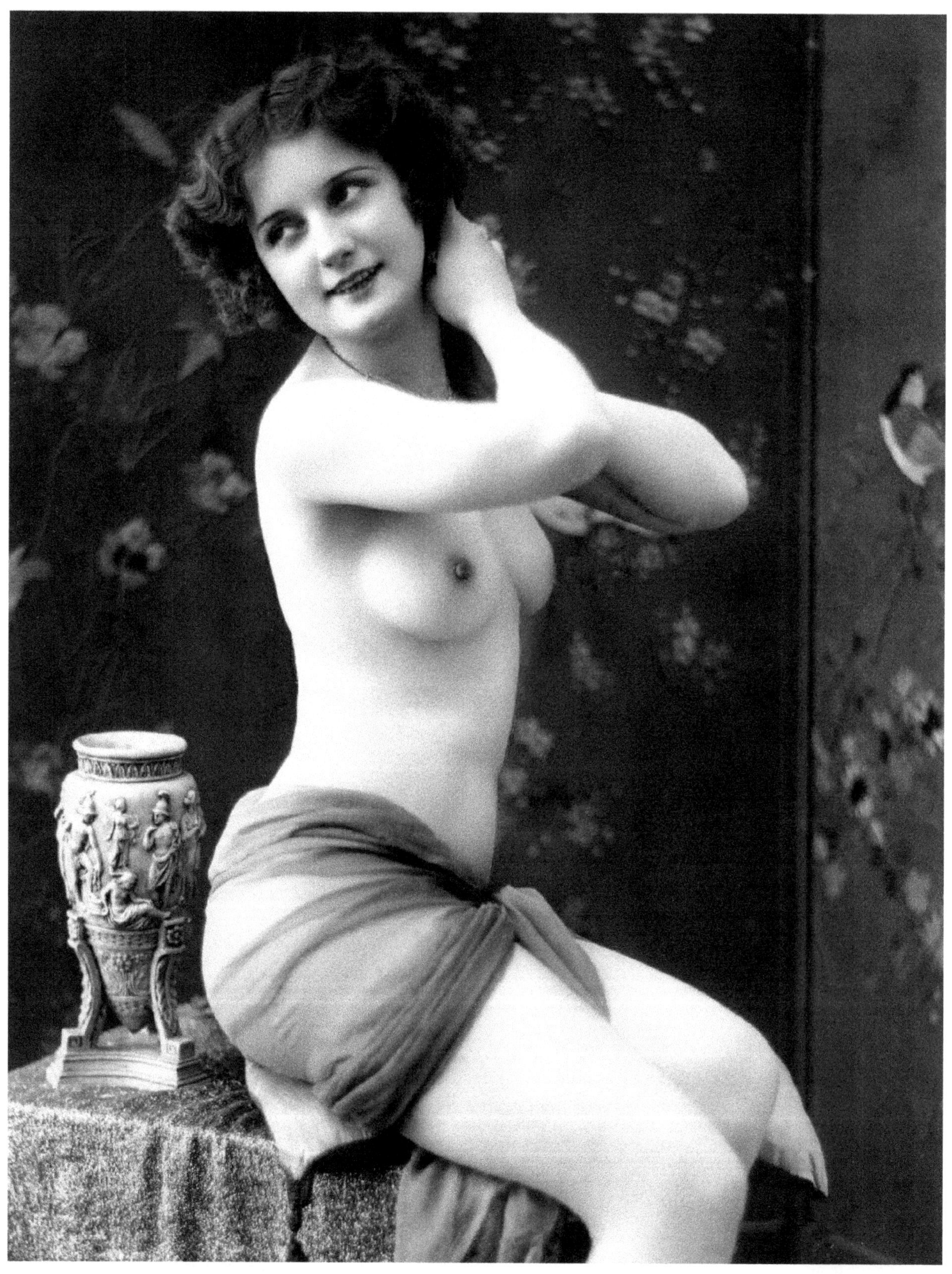

Nude Woman With Scarf

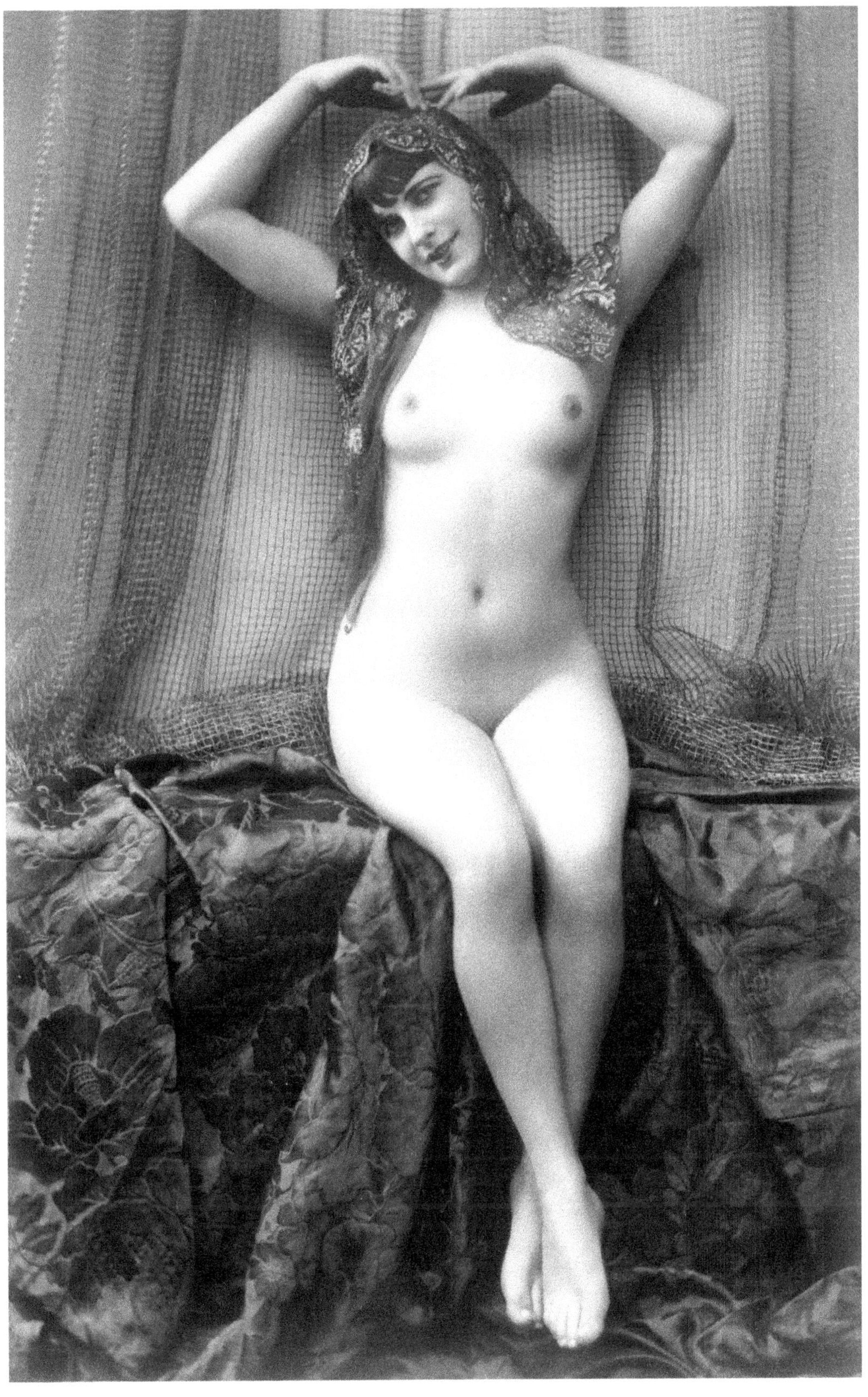

Nude Woman In Animal Fur

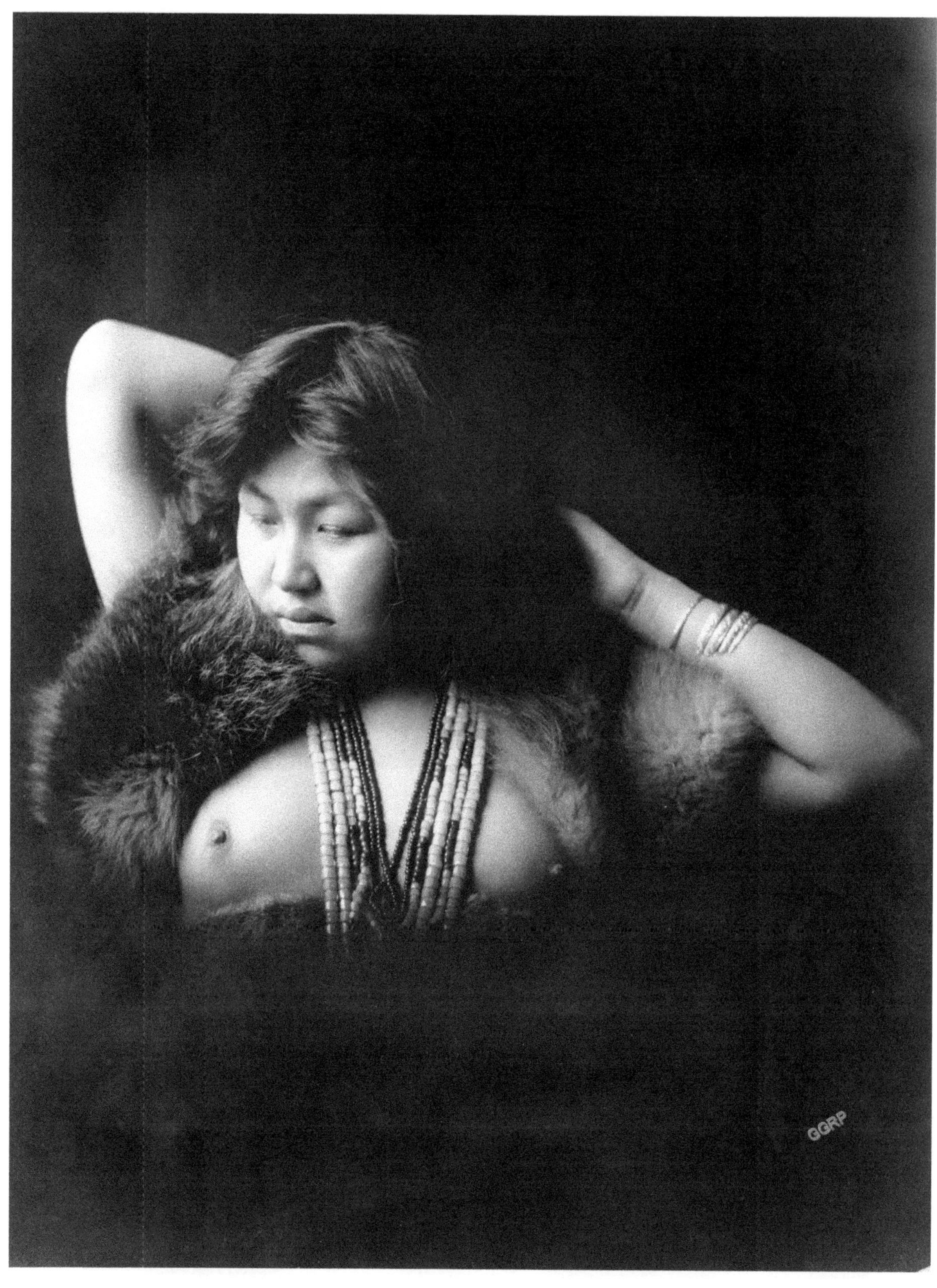

Nude Woman From Behind With Dirty Feet

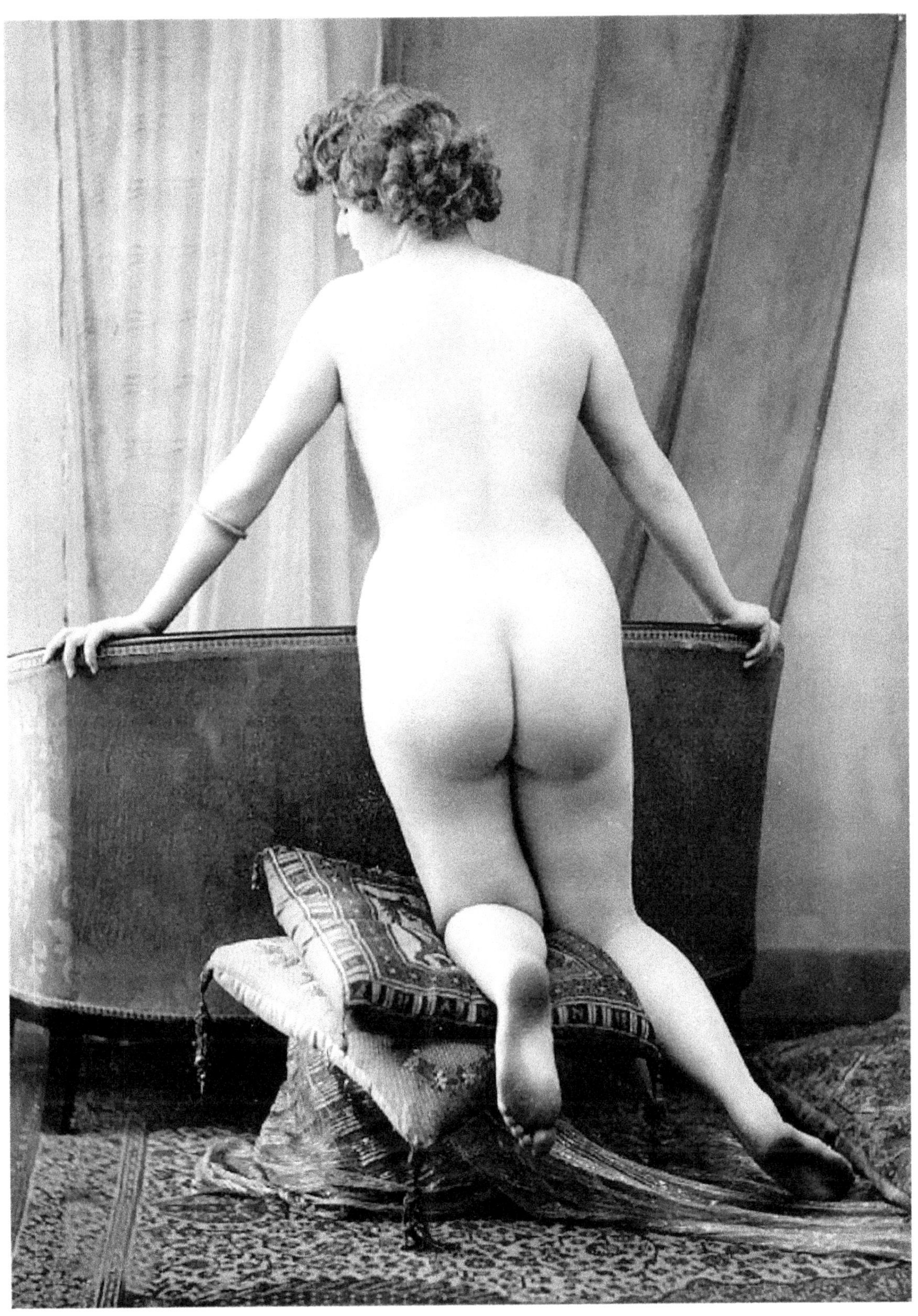

Nude Woman With Bright Smile

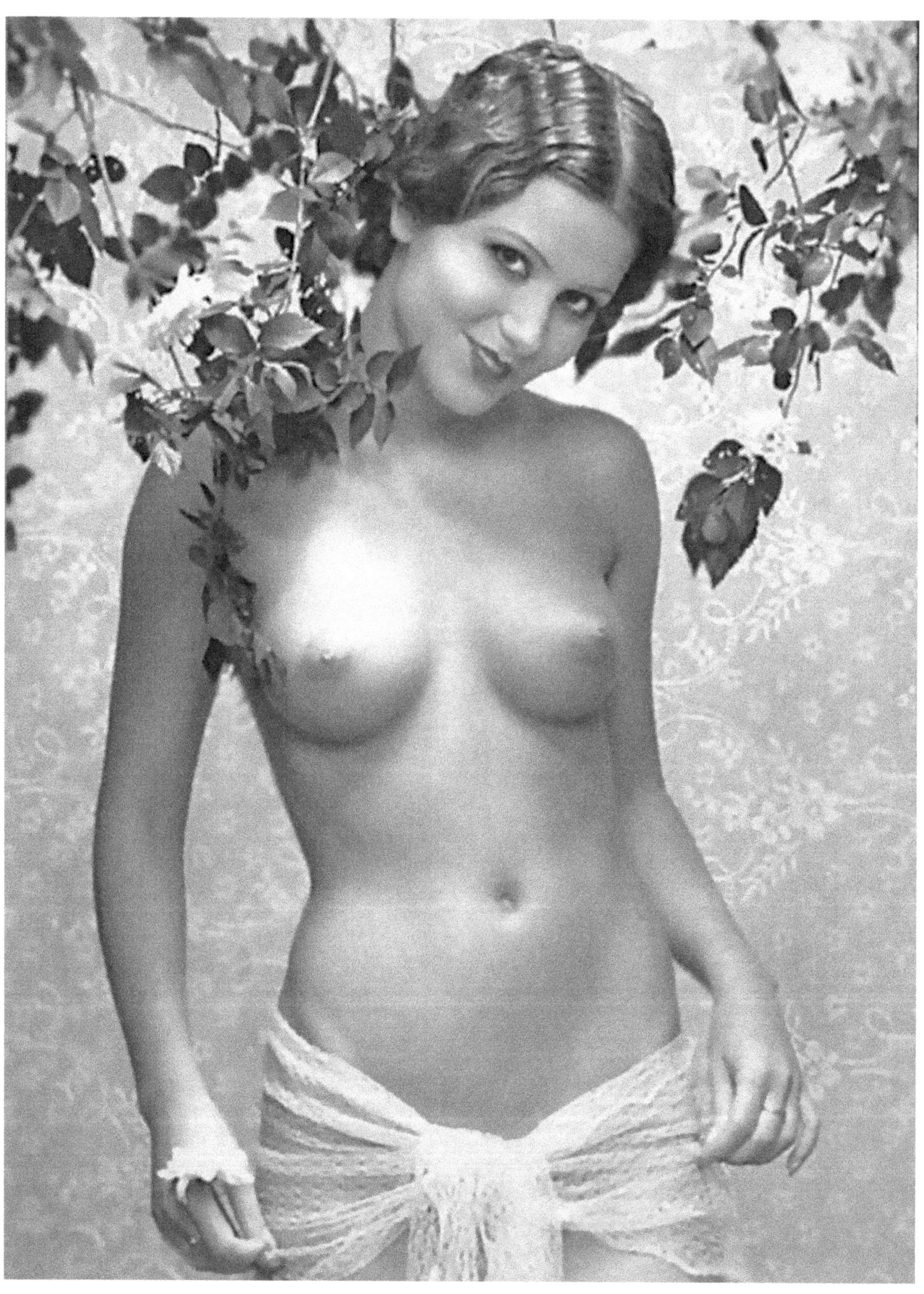

Nude Woman With Hand Mirror

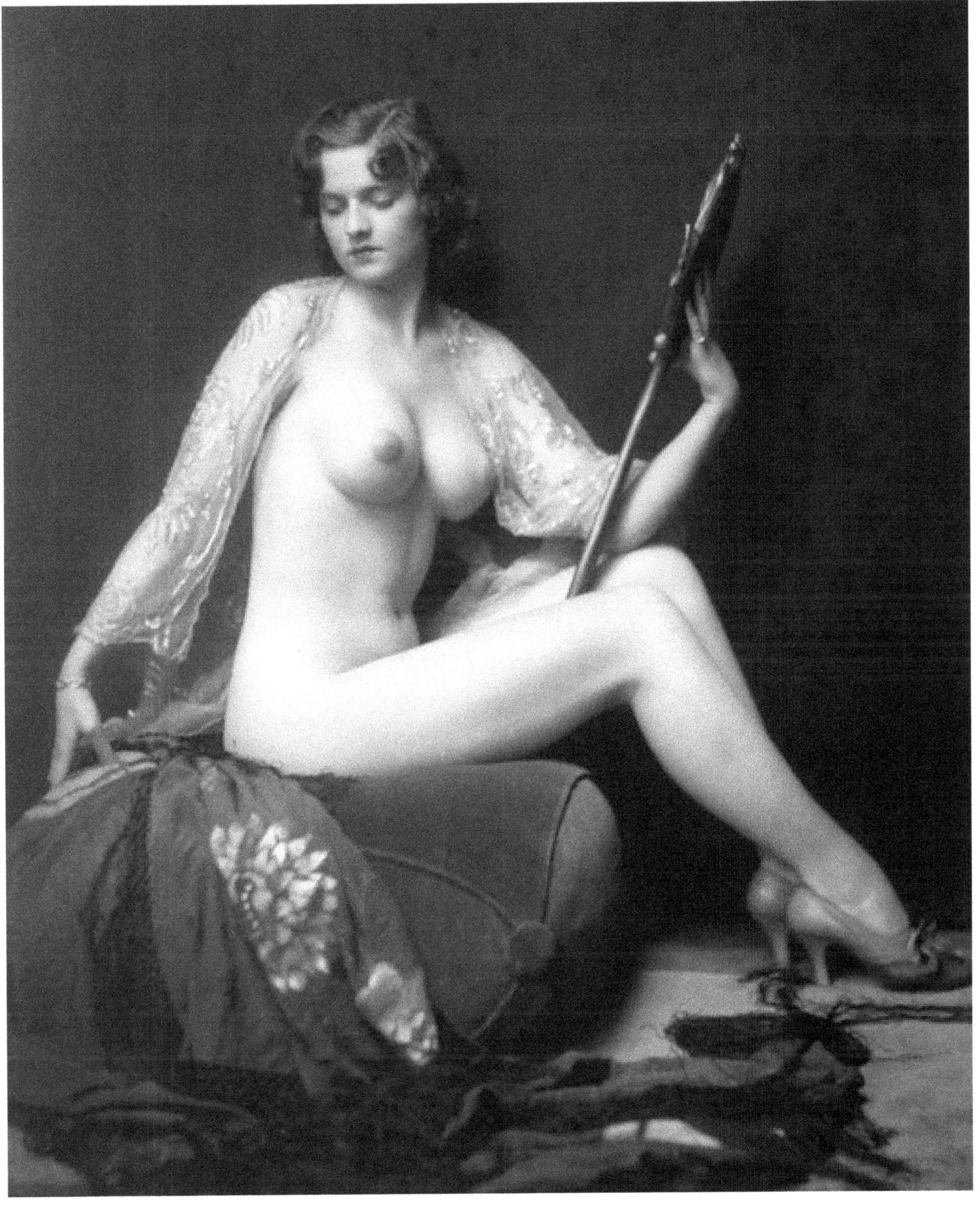

Nude Woman Posed By Mirror

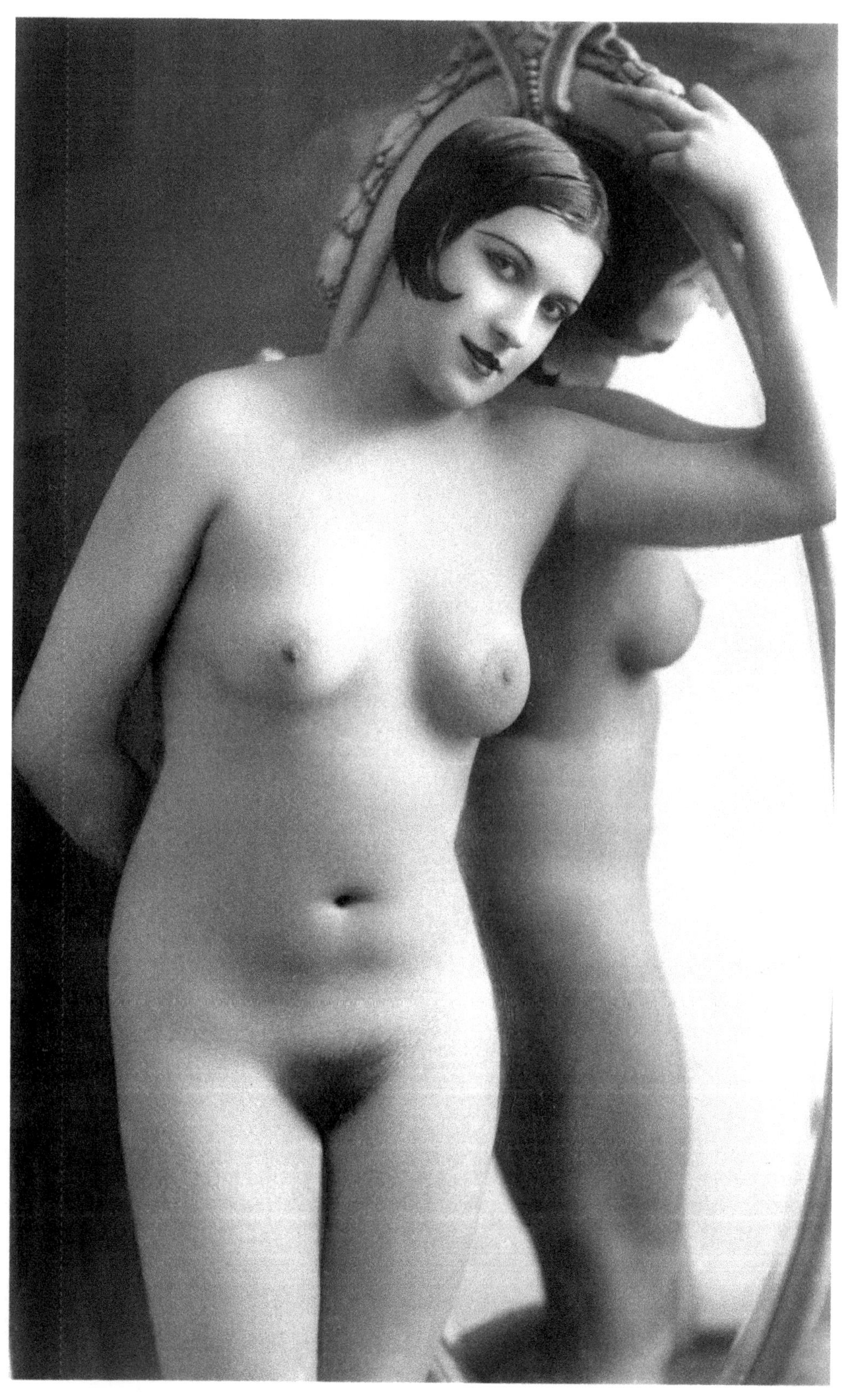

Nude Woman Admiring Herself in Hand Mirror

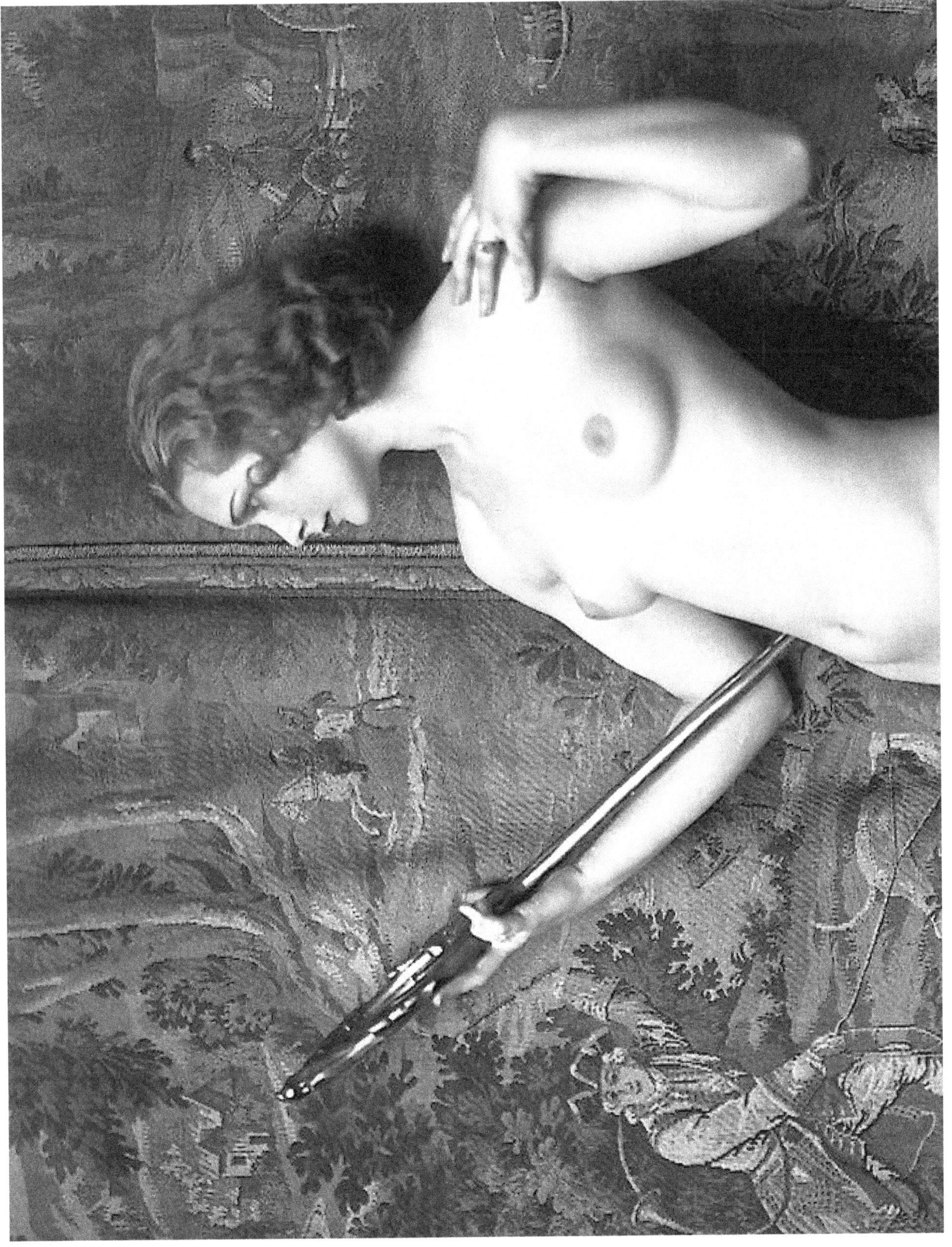

Nude Woman Looking At Vase

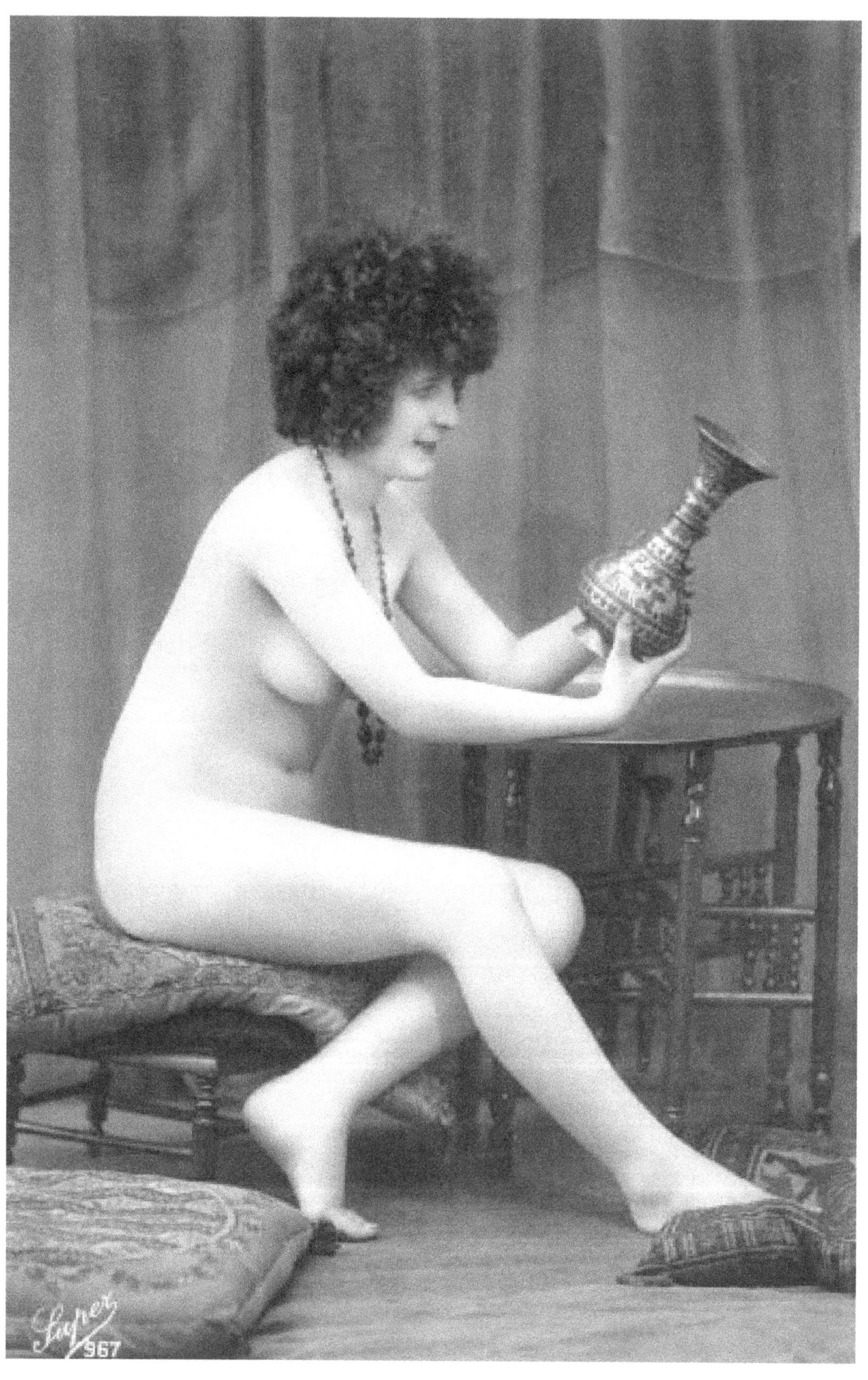

Nude Woman of Algiers

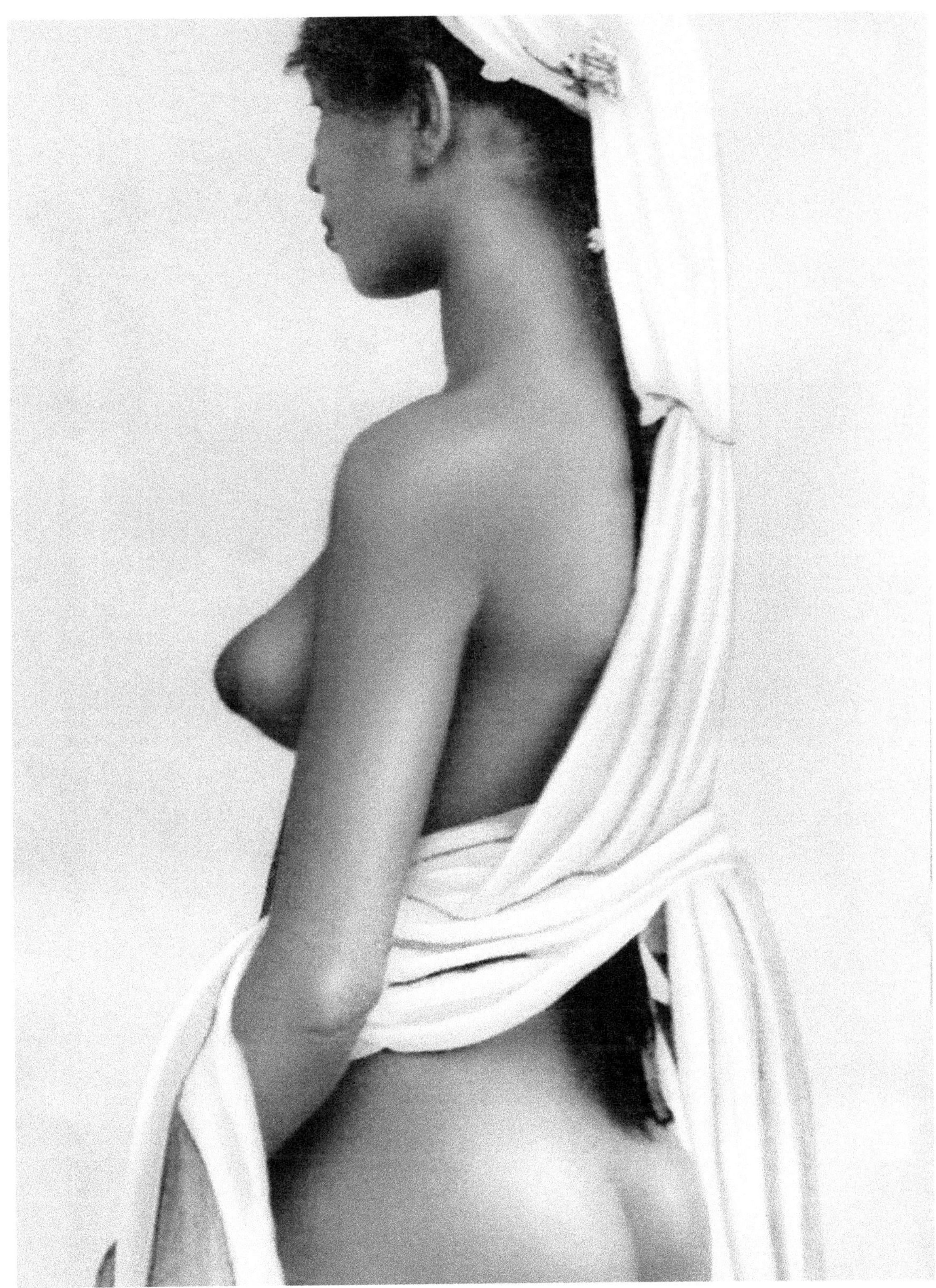

Nude Woman With Hand At Breast

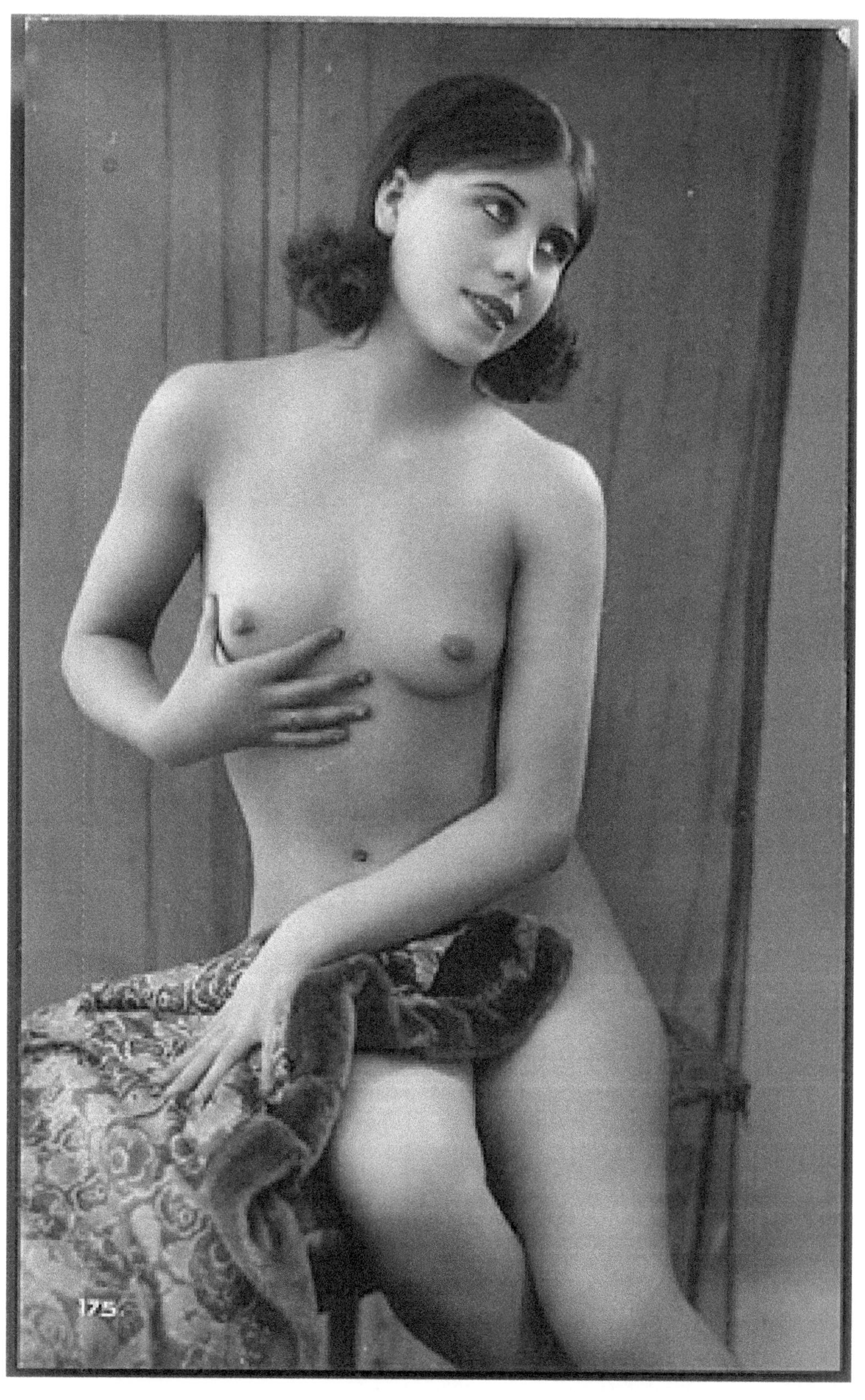

Nude Woman Lounging

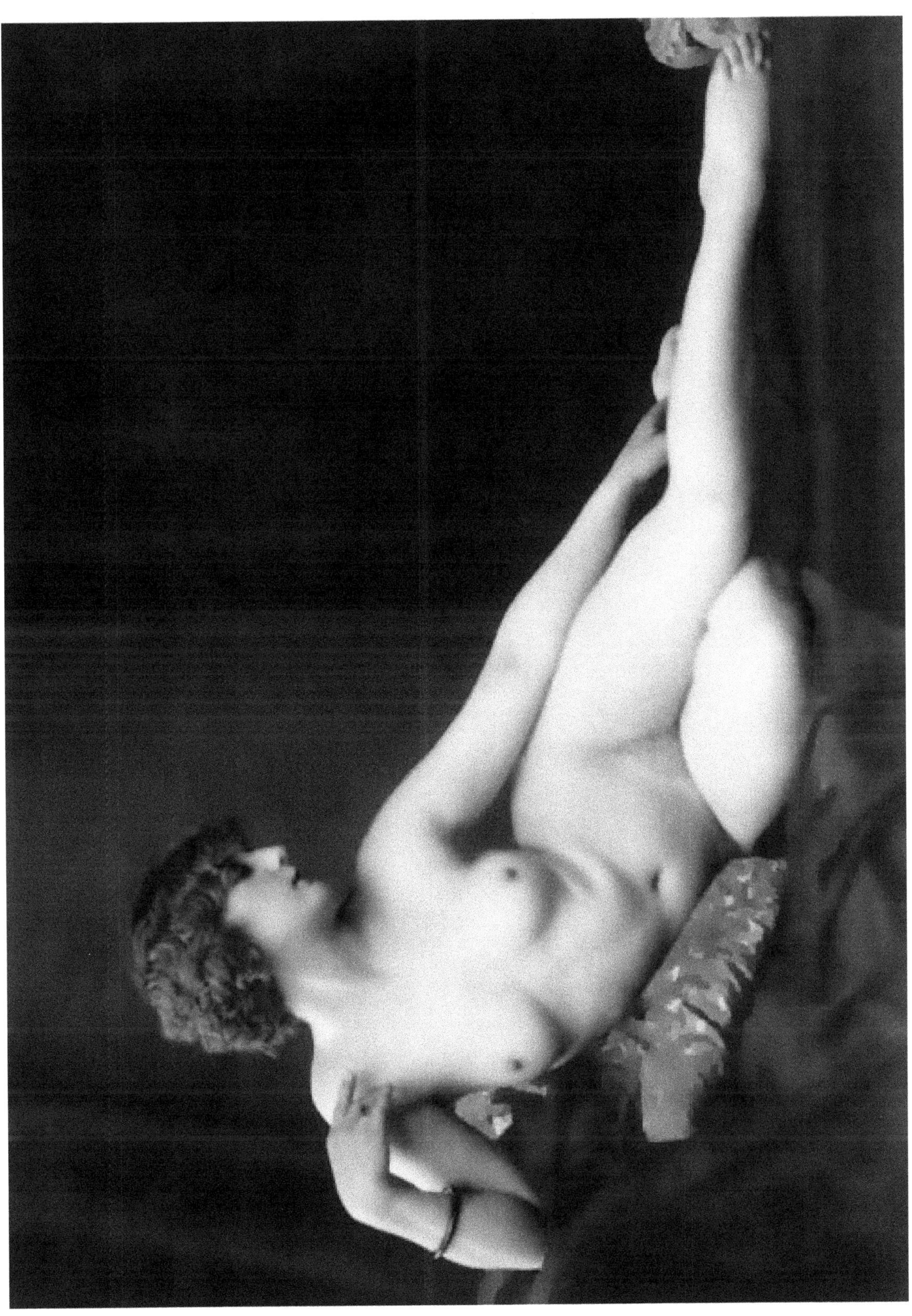

Nude Woman Stretching Arms

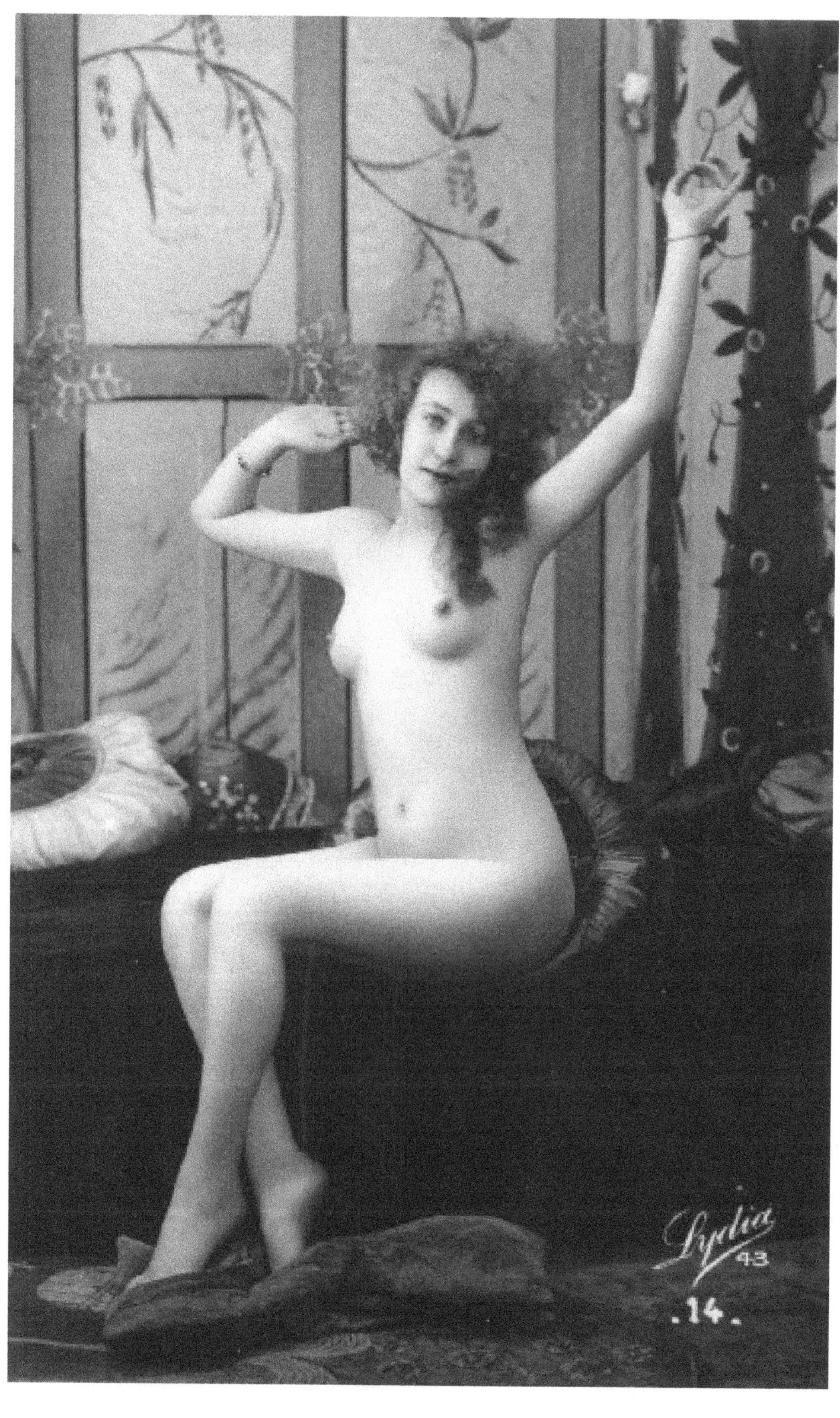

Nude Woman Full Frontal With Long Hair

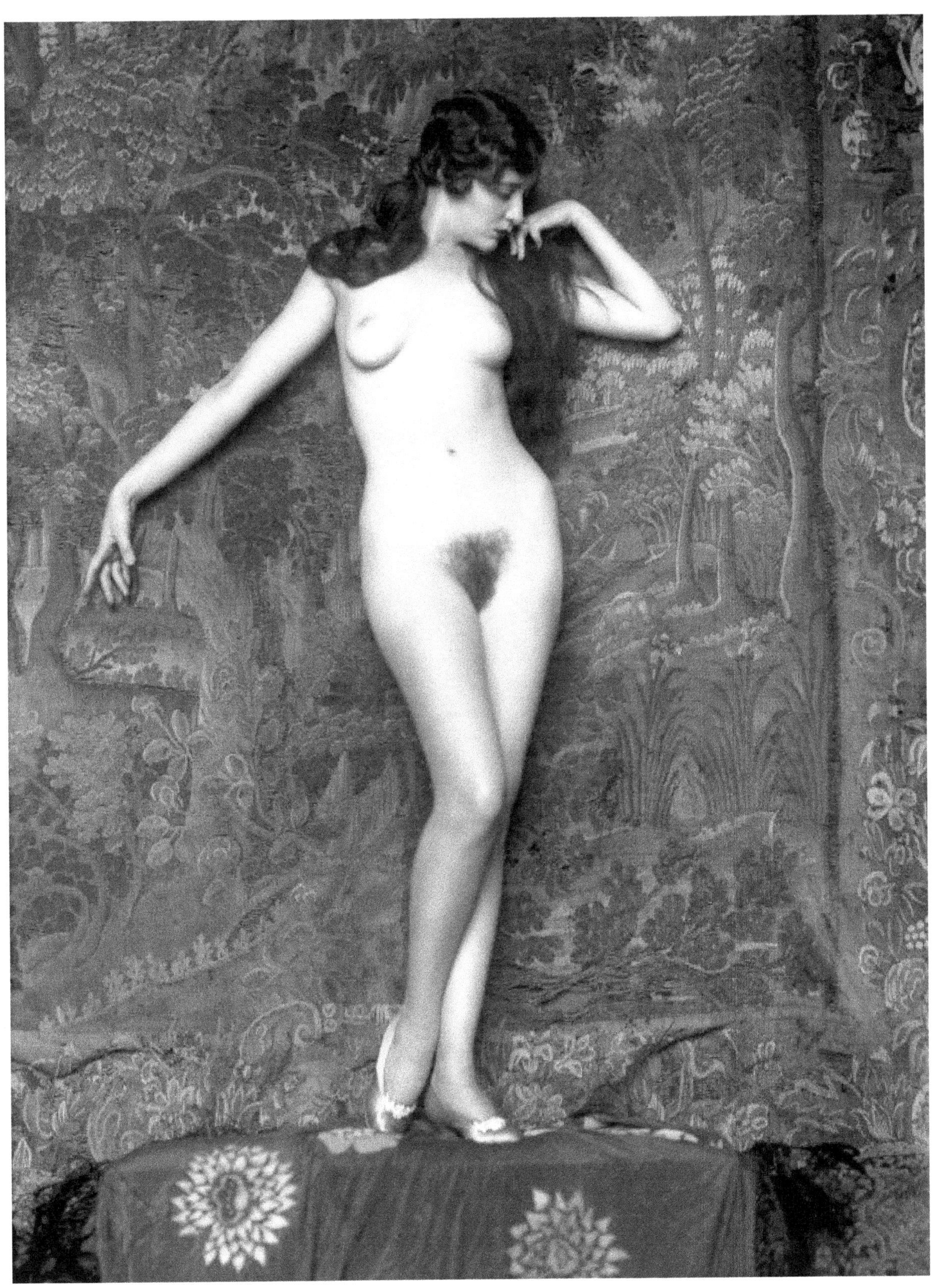

Nude Woman With Hoop

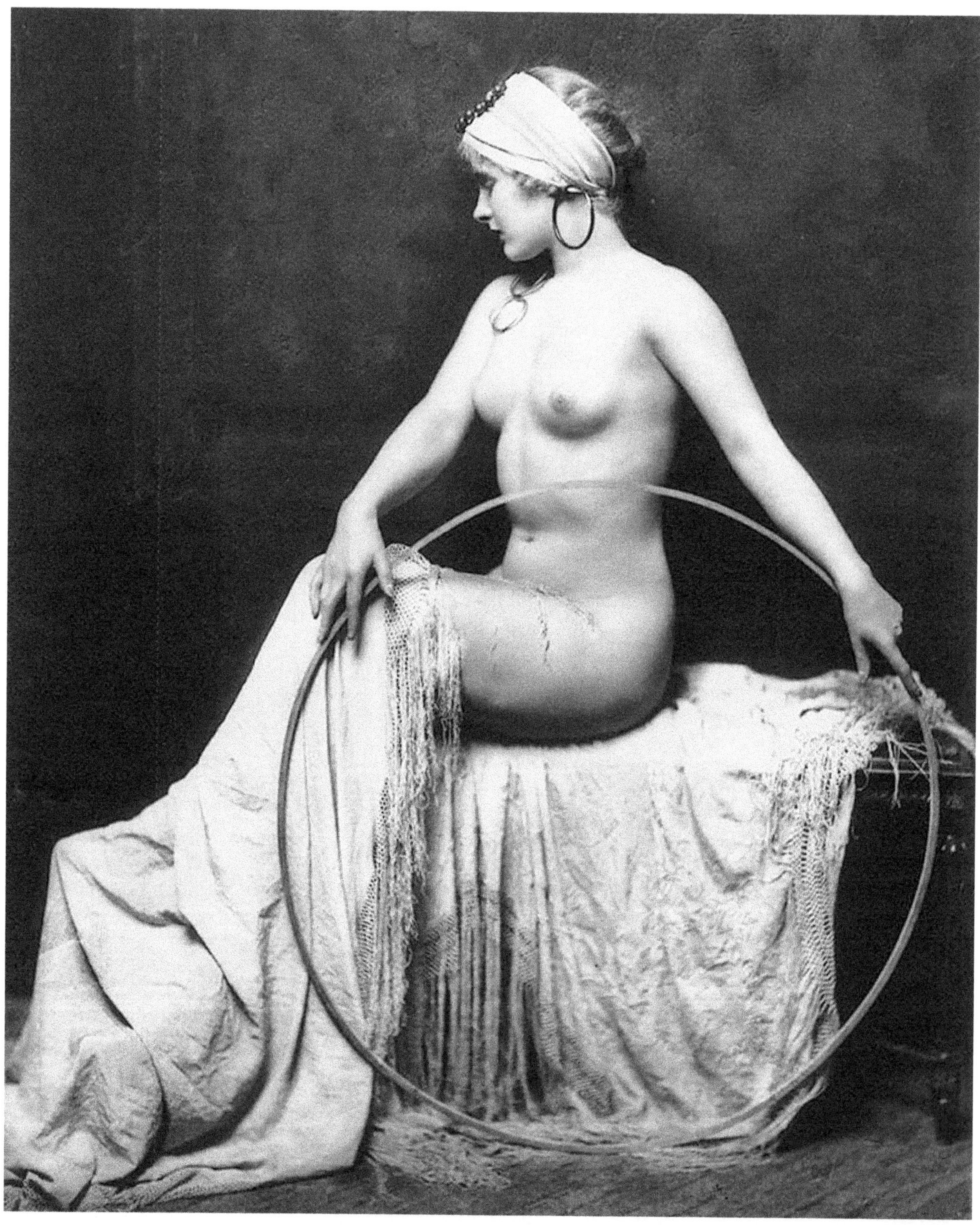

Nude Woman Pressed Against Mirror

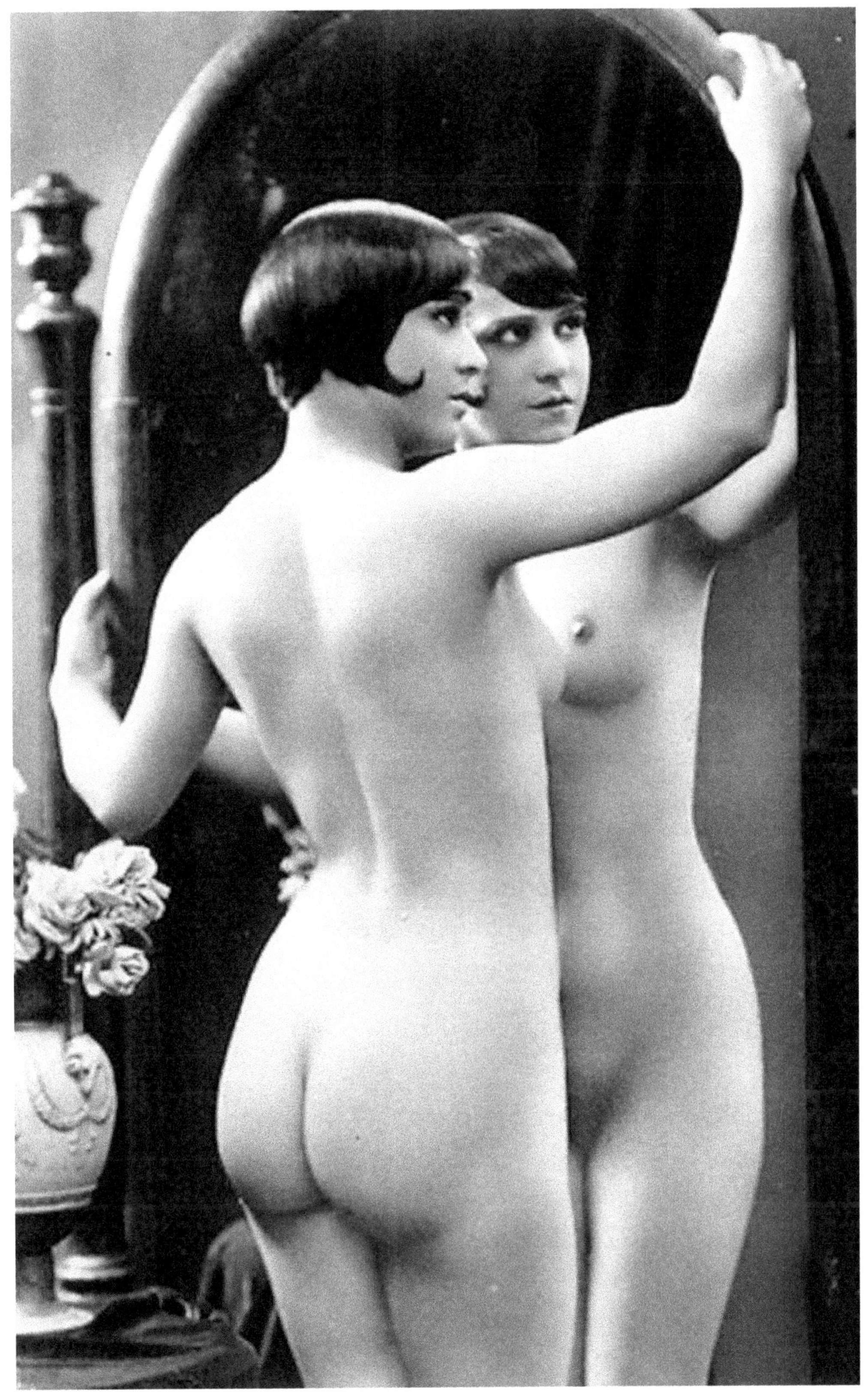

About The Author

Carl Scott Harker currently lives in a small coastal town in Southern Oregon where, along with pursuing writing projects, he runs a small photography business.

Mr. Harker is the author of several books including another pictorial featuring images of beautiful women entitled: ***"Classic Fine Art Nudes: Volume One."*** This book is available on Amazon at https://www.amazon.com/Classic-Fine-Art-Nudes-One/dp/1093912073.

Other Books by the Author

"Poems By My Cat" - a cycle of cat poems of action and wisdom. Here is the link to the book on Amazon here: https://www.amazon.com/Poems-Cat-Carl-Scott-Harker/dp/1793903239.

"100 Classic Poems To Read At Christmas Time" - an anthology of classic Christmas poems. The link to the book on Amazon is: https://www.amazon.com/dp/B07J9YS7QK.

"Seeds of Poetry: 21 Methods to Inspire Your Poetry and Other Creative Writings" - expand your creative writings and poetry with these methods. The link is: https://www.amazon.com/Seeds-Poetry-Methods-Creative-Writings/dp/1798587599/.

"Exploring The Universe: The Art of Space" - Through the use of instruments such as the Hubble Space Telescope, scientists have captured the colorful art that space itself creates. Here is the link: https://www.amazon.com/Exploring-Universe-Carl-Scott-Harker-ebook/dp/B077XQRPQL

www.ingramcontent.com/pod-product-compliance
Ingram Content Group UK Ltd.
Pitfield, Milton Keynes, MK11 3LW, UK
UKHW051207260726
13967UKWH00011B/3151

9 781070 440231